D1336703

Donegal Islands

Wallace Clark and Ros Harvey

Cottage
Publications

First published by Cottage Publications,
an imprint of Laurel Cottage Ltd.
Donaghadee, N. Ireland 2003.
Copyrights Reserved.
© Illustrations by Ros Harvey 2003.
© Text by Wallace Clark 2003.
All rights reserved.
No part of this book may be reproduced or stored on any media
without the express written permission of the publishers.
Design & origination in Northern Ireland.
Printed & bound in Singapore.
ISBN 1 900935 31 7

Ros Harvey

Ros Harvey was born and grew up in Malin on Inishowen, and spent her childhood 'messing about in boats' along the spectacular coastline of Donegal.

Ros had been a leading potter in Dublin for twelve years until a back operation stopped her working in that medium. She then moved into painting using soft pastels. She finds the tactile qualities of pastels a natural transition from clay.

The advantage of these pure colours enable her to recreate the fast changing light and atmosphere of this northern coast.

She has exhibited her paintings and prints in England, Germany, Holland, Italy and the U.S., as well as at the annual Academy exhibitions in Belfast and Dublin and at the Royal Society of Marine Artists in London.

Donegal Islands is a natural follow on to *Inishowen*, an earlier best seller in this series which Ros also illustrated.

Wallace Clark

Wallace Clark is a linen manufacturer by trade and a sailor by inclination. He has been making friends in the Donegal islands by visits in boats varying from currachs to galleys, dinghies and cutters since 1948.

His sailing interests cover the spectrum from leisure sailing to participating in several research projects to explore the seafaring technology of bygone times.

These included a currach voyage from Derry to Iona in 1963, participation on Tim Severin's Brendan Voyage across the Atlantic in 1977 and the Lord of the Isles Voyage when Wallace oversaw the construction of the first Highland Galley in 300 years and her voyage from Westport to Stornoway.

Drawing on this rich experience he has written a number of books about sailing and islands including: *Rathlin – Its Island Story; The Lord of the Isles Voyage; Sailing Round Russia* and, perhaps his best known book, *Sailing Round Ireland* which is regarded as a classic of its kind.

The Wish of the Wise:–

> *A boat to sail in,*
> *A sea to sail over,*
> *An island to sail to,*
> *And the wish never to leave it.*

Anon.

From the flyleaf of a book
found on the Isle of Gigha.

Islands fascinate. Irish islands fascinate more than most and this book will introduce you to a couple of dozen of her most alluring.

It has been my good fortune to become familiar with all of them during voyages in sailing boats from 1950 until the present day. Ros Harvey, my cousin and illustrator, joined me on some of the early visits and latterly to all the isles.

How could one fail to fall in love with islets when they charm all the senses? The smell of peat smoke as you ghost in under sail in the darkness before dawn, the salty tangle of seaweed at low tide, the brilliant smell of water as you fill your lungs with an ozonic wind, purified by hundreds of miles of Atlantic Ocean.

For your eyes there is the reflectivity of the surrounding sea which gives island atmospheres a clarity that can make objects five miles away appear close at hand. Thongs of seaweed sparkle like footlights as they coil and uncoil in a low swell under the esoteric light of Irish coastal skies with their faint elusive yellow tinge.

For your ears there is the rustle of the surf … a low murmur, always changing, always the same, *'the sound of the sound of the sea.'*

For the touch there is the goodly feel of smooth stone, or sheep-cropped grass under bare feet. But don't sit on island grass in September or the bites of Orange Tawneys will make you itch for days. A morning plunge into seawater warmed just a little by the Gulf Stream makes your body glow for hours.

Visiting islands is about people. Islanders have more time to think than us mainlanders. That makes them shrewd commentators on events they observe across water. They need a variety of skills – many an islander is a farmer, boat builder, engineer, stonemason and electrician as well as a master of the essential art of fishing. You learn a lot in the company of such people.

5

where you take them. If disapproving they drop bits of gear overboard and become slow at answering the helm.

Other visits have been in currachs. The Irish currach can claim a unique construction and design unchanged for two thousand years. Essentially it consists of a framework of thin pliable laths or withies over which are stretched animal hide or a woven fabric coated in tar. The primaeval requirements were for a craft which could be built without a saw mill or forge, in places where timber was scarce. She had to be light enough to be carried ashore on open beaches or rocky islands where no harbour existed. These have not changed and the currach survives. To anyone who enjoys small boat handling the currach yields a particular pleasure, in its ability to ride over waves in the fashion of a swimming seagull.

And the thinness of its skin gives one a feeling of being in touch with the works of the Lord and His wonders in the deep to a degree never quite equalled in a planked boat. The added advantage of being able to turn a currach upside down and sleep under her at night makes a boat ideal for the Rosses of Donegal.

When, in the following pages, *'we'* are mentioned as landing here or anchoring there, the reference is to shipmates too numerous to introduce individually, with whom I've been lucky enough to go to sea – most often my wife June, my cousin Ros, the most amiable of artists; with our respective

A Desert Isle may fascinate in storybooks. In real life inhabited islands are more stimulating. *Ireland of the Welcomes* lives up to its name better among island communities than almost anywhere else – kindness comes in many forms from every hand. Four of those we'll visit in the following pages have year round communities. Others are lonely cemeteries of ships which have been wrecked on their protective fangs of rock. Some of the most enjoyable are the kingdoms of fish, crabs and lobsters, gulls and stormy petrels.

Owey and Umfin have echoing caverns penetrating red cliffs. Three others have traces of Neolithic occupation and nine have evidence of sixth century monks. Most islets have sandy bays where you can stretch out in the sun and you used to be able hear the click of oars round the point. Now, sadly, it is more likely to be the roar of an outboard engine. A few isles have plantations of trees. Here and there you find the natural rockbound harbours that are so much more agreeable to boats than concrete boxes or marinas. Yes, to boats!

May I introduce my islander ones? Five in number – *San Ferian*, an 18 foot gunter-rigged half decker, *Caru*, a 27 foot mahogany sloop, *Zamorin*, a 60 year old gaff cutter, *Wild Goose*, a 35 foot yawl built in 1934 and, at present, *Agivey*, a 32 foot plastic ketch. These yachts have been fitted out at home with the help of friends, never in yards and all have personalities. They let you know in subtle ways if they like relations and friends – Tim, Terry, Billy, Chris, Davy, Ricky, John, Steven, Willie, Lewis, Milo, and and and …

Thanks also from Ros and me to the skilled boatmen who got us to islands when the book was being prepared – Charlie and George from Malin Head, Jimmy Sweeny to Tory, Jim Boyd and Willie Sweeny from Bunbeg, Roger to Rathlin O'Birne and Rodney Lomax to Inishmurray.

If you sit quietly in an old ship, especially a wooden one, and listen in the right way you can sometimes get an echo off her well-used timbers of the jokes and stories, talk and tale, beef and beer, that have made many good evenings round her cabin table. So writing this book has brought back for me, and I hope will evoke for others, many wonderful memories.

The variety of our islands is remarkable, yet all in common face the wide Atlantic. Let's go and have a look at them.

7

Inishtrahull

Garvans

Glashedy

Tory

Inishdooey & Inishbóffin

Inishsirrer & Inishmeane

Umfin & Gola

Owey

Aranmore   Rutland, Eighter & Inishcoo

Inishkeeragh   Inishfree

Inishkeel

Roanish

Rathlin O'Birne

Inishmurray

Lough Erne

Contents

1. Inishtrahull, the Garvans and Glashedy

The first group of islands we shall visit lies close around Ireland's north point. There the isles are exposed to the full force of gales from east and west as well as north. Additionally tidal streams, much stronger than those on the west, when opposed to quite moderate winds, add an extra hazard by making waves taller and steeper. A magnificent spectacle for the watcher on shore but the small boat skipper must forever work closely with fair tides and know where to find shelter in the lee of jagged rocks.

Inishtrahull

'Inishtrahull was not a lonely place at all.'

Edward McCarron, lightkeeper 1872

The Hull, as the island is locally known, stands at the apex of Ireland, five miles northeast of Malin Head. The most isolated and ancient of all our inhabited isles, it is formed mainly of hard lewisian gneiss. This rock formed the last land bridge between Ireland and Scotland which remained intact until melting ice raised sea levels about 8000 years ago. That put a stop to the procession of cave bears, mammoths, elk and their like which passed this way from con-

tinental Europe into Ireland. Inishtrahull must have been a sort of Noah's staging point on the way without Noah. Luckily for the animals, man was still some thousands of years astern. What a peaceful Eden Ireland must have been minus *Homo sapiens.*

Monks came to the Hull early in the Christian era soon after 500 A.D. They left some visible traces but the name of the associated saint or abbot has been forgotten as there is no written record of their time on the island.

I guess Inishtrahull was inhabited most summers from then on except in periods when piracy made it too risky, for it has the best natural harbour of any Donegal island and seven good wells. Hence it was an almost essential port of call for small boats or currachs bound coastwise or from the west of Ireland to the Hebrides.

By the 18th Century the island had an established community. By one account in 1850, as mainland population pressures increased, this rose to an incredible 400. A hundred seems a more likely figure. They would have lived on fish and sea birds and were able to grow a few acres of barley and keep a few sheep, but by this time there was a chance to trade.

Sailing ships were often held up by a foul wind or tide. The watchful islanders would row out to sell turbot to be landed in Liverpool next day, trade poteen for rope or sailcloth, land stowaways at a fee of a pound a head or accept smuggled 'baccy' to be passed on to the mainland. In the days of steam trawlers mutton was swapped for coal.

So Inishtrahull was more dependant than perhaps any other Irish island on contacts with passing ships. The island boat crews in the 1920s were described to me as 'wild raw-boned men in homespun wool with hair down their back and beards to their waists'.

My first acquaintance with the Hull was in June 1948. That was only twenty years after the permanent population had left. My cousin

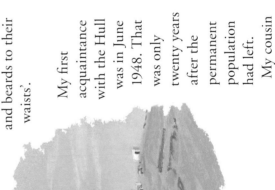

Inishtrahull Light

Roland and I shared an 18-foot half decker called *San Ferian* and were on passage east after visiting Sheephaven.

Seeing the twin humps and lighthouse of the island clear abeam we decided to try to fetch it for the night. As soon as we turned the tide did the same and cold Irish Sea water mingling with the Gulf Stream produced a fog. We could see barely 50 yards. The wind dropped. A four-horse-power Seagull outboard mounted abeam (it wouldn't fit on our long counter stern) enabled us to carry on by compass. Frequently it was necessary to stop the engine and listen for the horn – two blasts every 30 seconds – and correct our course for possible cross-tides.

After fifty anxious minutes steep rocks, yellow with lichen, appeared ahead followed by a shadowy figure, its arm pointing left. The shadow followed us as we reached the east of the island and made a hundred and eighty degree turn round a point. Then we found ourselves in a circular tide rip which made *San Ferian* take what was later described as a 'tremendjous lep'. Suddenly there was a calm silvery creek ahead and a concrete jetty topped by a wooden crane.

All landfalls are exciting but this was one of my most memorable. More so because it gave an insight into what must have happened to island boats in the past; boats with no compass, no engine and no horn to guide them in. Maybe only a barking dog or a tin can beaten by anxious folk ashore.

Portmore, Inishtrahull

'It is a melancholy fact that nearly all the island men met their deaths by drowning', wrote Edward McCarron who worked on the island in 1870.

"We thought you were a disabled seaplane motoring in", said our guide who we soon got to know as Ed Meehan, the Principal Keeper. I think he was a bit disappointed at our wee boat's insignificance. His remark showed the extraordinary way in which the fog and the resonance of our wooden hull had magnified the sound of our four-horse engine. Two more keepers, Frank McCarthy and William Coupe, appeared and took lines to moor us safe in the middle of the weed-draped creek.

Soon we found ourselves being entertained to tea by three men at the Horn Station. Each man had his own bread, butter and sugar and pushed them in turn towards us. That was standard Irish Lights practice to avoid friction over appetites when crews were confined together for weeks. The P.K. insisted on giving us beds in the room of a man on leave but I don't remember sleeping much. The roar of the horn every 30 seconds seemed powerful enough to make the very mattress vibrate. But, hell, we were young and would sleep it off at home next day.

Light keepers were famed for their hospitality and they are nowadays sadly missed on the islands. Inishtrahull was automated in 1987, and now only periodic visits for maintenance are required.

In the morning the fog had gone and the horn was silent at last. We could see below us the few acres of tillage so low that in winter gales the sea breaks right across at high water. The island is about a mile long by half a mile wide, something like a comma, with the port facing east in the nick on the north side. A dozen houses, mostly roofless, could still be counted with the larger schoolhouse on a rise to our left.

The keepers were asleep after their night watches so we stole out to explore. We found in the lee of Craignahull, the hill which arises mid island, a rude half circle of stones which served as an open-air church. The islanders were most devout Catholics and would not think of going to sea without 'a wee mouthful of prayer' and a bottle of holy water in the bow.

Like so many Irish islands the Hull had its monastery but no details have survived. Perhaps, as in early Saga records of the Papa or Irish monks on Iceland, 'when the Vikings arrived the holy men went away'. Visible traces are no more than an altar stone with an incised Cross and the bases of two beehive huts just east of the pier. Boats needing ballast removed the stones within living memory.

A dolmen with capstone, perhaps from even earlier days, lines up with the Tor Rocks out to the north and the sunrise on particular dates making an effective almanac indicating perhaps when to put the ram out with the ewes and when the lambs might be expected. Edible snails, *Helix Aspersa*, eaten in huge quantities in France today are still to be found near the seven wells and were probably brought here to vary the diet of the monks.

In 1948 on the east hill opposite us stood the Light manned by another three keepers. It was only in the 1970s, as labour became more expensive, that the light and horn were amalgamated and the present graceful steel tower erected beside the horn.

We found in a north-facing hollow beyond the light a ring of stones surrounding a pathetic graveyard. Its wooden crosses marked the bodies of light keeper's children and islanders alike but today no names are decipherable.

A bathe in a shallow creek just north of Craignahull finished the exploration. We had been told that it is warmed by an eddy of the Gulf Stream. It still seemed icy to me, but worth it for the glow afterwards as we dried ourselves in a bed of white mayweed by the water's edge.

The five-hour passage home to Porrush that afternoon was over a calm blue Atlantic with Islay and Jura clear to port. I have sailed to Inishtrahull many times since and been shown fresh secrets like Stack Mannanon, sacred to the King of the Sea; Virgin with cowl; the Pillar of the Grey Man; the Smugglers Hole and the house of Biddy McGonigle, Queen of the island, its rafters made from ships

timbers fastened with tapered oak trenails. Many more traces of earlier occupants must still lie undiscovered.

Much island lore and sea wisdom came from talks with Charlie 'Tacker' who after the island was evacuated in 1928 lived in Portaleen. His nickname was derived from the sailing skill that meant he would rather tack his boat twenty times than row a hundred yards. His longevity, well into the eighties, proved as a neighbour remarked, that Guinness is good for you, especially in large quantities. A great man.

There's always something new to see on Inishtrahull, a green haven for small boats in mid ocean. For all its tiny size it has a feel of urgency as befits a vital staging point for birds and men on their way to remote destinations.

The Garvans

The three Garvan Islands and their flotilla of rocks and reefs extend like stepping-stones from Ireland's north point towards Inishtrahull and Scotland. It is a mini-archipelago which has an evil reputation. Set athwart the tidal streams like the famous Bitches (the spiky rampart which half-fill the Sound of Ramsay Island off Wales) they have collected their share of wrecks.

A First World War destroyer was lost there in 1918. There have been recent fishing boat disasters. Coast dwellers tend to advise that landing is impossible – the sort of remark that makes anyone who loves islands want to have a go.

There is an excellent new slip at Malin Head Harbour two miles east of the Head. Ros, Tim and I launched our fourteen-foot dinghy there and a five-horse power outboard took us out in 15 minutes. But it is no place to go boating for beginners. *In no part of the world do such sudden and extraordinary changes in the weather take place*, thunders an old Admiralty Pilot.

We had picked slack water to get across. There will be many mentions of tides in the following pages as they so vitally affect island life, so some explanation seems appropriate. The flood tide, when fishes start to feed, rises for about six and a quarter hours and the ebb follows for the same period. This means that high water occurs about an hour later on each successive day. Slack water, meaning an easement and reversal of tidal streams, usually coincides with high and low water. Highest and lowest tides known as Springs occur about three days after each full and new moon, and Neaps, when movements are less, half way between. The Spring rise in Donegal is up to 13 feet.

Green Island, the first we came to, is the highest of the group. Shaped like a 65 foot high limpet shell, it has green grass showing at most times of the year. Sloping, weed-draped rocks all round make landing risky, especially at low water, but at high tide you can usually scramble ashore dry-shod. Sensible seagulls that prefer soil to rocks for rearing their chicks love nesting on Green Island.

Next comes Middle Island. You've passed Rossnabarton and Carrick-na-dreelyagh. Scararony and Carrickbane lie ahead – names that sound like a bar of music. Why these flat English titles Green, Middle and White? They are almost the only islets with non-Gaelic names on the coast. Was it just the whim of a surveyor or a landlord who had no Irish? I have not been able to discover.

Middle Island has a 10 foot cliff on its north side with plenty of footholds and enough depth to float a boat at low water. It's as dinky a wee boat port as you'd find in a day. With good fenders you can tie your boat alongside and be protected by a couple of isolated rocks close by. But only in calm, settled weather.

that poteen makers set up their stills here in the past. This local equivalent of whiskey is pronounced 'potyeen' and varies in quality from excellent to eye-blinding jungle juice. Perhaps it was the distiller's wish to pursue their honest trade undisturbed by Customs or Garda that caused word to be spread that the Garvan Islands are impossible to land on. It was of course essential for the distillers to sample the brew frequently as it trickled warm out of the still and seagull's eggshells made handy glasses.

White Island is next in line, named after a cliff, white from bird droppings. There is a landing for the agile on the west side but take it easy. A crew member of mine failed to leap the gap and fell into deep water. It was a job getting him out. A similar experience was aptly described in *The Ballad of Sir Patrick Spens*:—

Laith, laith, were the good Scots lairds
To wet their cork heeled shoon.
But lang afore the play was played
They'd wet their hats aboon.

It was near White Island that the *Racoon* foundered. She was heading west for the Swilly in a northerly gale on the long night of January 1918, one of a pair of destroyers employed as convoy escort, under orders to return to their mother ship *HMS Hecla* in Lough Swilly. A snowstorm blotted out Inishtrahull light and reduced visibility to less than 50 yards. About 2am she struck a rock just beyond White

In May the upper rocks of Middle are alive with seabirds; cormorants on messy nests of dried seaweed, full of young sticking up necks like black snakes; eider ducks who pull that famous down over their eggs to hide them before flying heavily off their nests; oyster catchers with the white cross of St Brigid on their backs who are able to carry their young to safety between their legs; rock pipits; herring gulls and half a dozen more.

There is a certain short-term benefit to the birds when humans are around because the smarter ones realise that, with hulky visitors nearby, the gulls will not strike. So they visibly relax but, as soon as they leave, robbers move in to eat unguarded eggs and chicks. May and June are months when human beings should not land other than briefly for serious observation.

In the centre of Middle Island is a hollow containing a brackish pool, fouled to a sickly green by the activities of gulls. But it could easily be cleaned out and the slope above is a good spot for a picnic. I feel rather envious of the fisherman called Andy McKergan, of the Portstewart family, who is remembered as camping hereabouts for weeks and drying his fish in summers long ago. McKerrigan's Bagh on the chart is a better memorial to his bold spirit than any arid tombstone.

A few bottles in a rocky niche told stories of other activities. None contained anything imbibable. But it seems likely

Island. A hundred yards further north she would have been as safe as her consort who did not even see her go down. Of *Racoon's* crew of 92, more than half were stokers clad in singlets in the boiler room. Their survival time in icy water would have been minutes. As she sank in 20 fathoms every man on board perished. Divers have recently found the remains and recovered parts of her forward gun.

An entry in a letter dated 18th April 1836 from Mr McHenry, the curate of Culdaff, illustrates the risks of fishing these waters.

On Easter Tuesday two boats left Malin Head with eight men in each. They were driven out to sea by the storm and could not make land before Friday morning. One got into Redford with five men lying dead in it, the other into Malin also with five dead. One of the survivors has since died and another lost his mind.

If you like small islands, and like 'em wild the Garvans are exciting places to visit but have an experienced skipper, go at neap tides and be careful. Otherwise you can get a fine view of them from the cliffs of Inishowen.

Glashedy

This islet lies boldly out in almost perpetual surf, three quarters of a mile off Carrickabraghy Castle on the Isle of Doagh. Carrickabraghy is no longer a castle – not the sort where you could drop in for a cup of coffee; just evocative ruins from which The O'Doherty of mediaeval days guarded his salmon fisheries in Strawbreagy – *Tra Breige*, the treacherous strand. A Viking silver hoard was found nearby so occupation began much earlier.

Doagh is no longer an island – as sea levels have fallen it has become joined to the shore by a square mile of saltings and meadows where Glashedy geese love to graze. This shoreline forms a fitting mainland to face a remarkable islet. It might have been designed as a trap for sailing ships attempting to round Malin Head but finding themselves a little too far south and unable to beat to windward out of it.

In 1602 the Danish bus *Dove* was wrecked on the Five Finger Strand and a huge catch of hake cod and turbot looted before the ship herself was hacked to pieces for timber.

The Harvey family of Malin Hall were publicly praised, at hundred year intervals, for taking a leading part in saving crews on the *Ebenezer* in 1778 and the *Danube* in 1878. A Harvey pleasure boat was launched from the rough slip just inshore of the castle to take off the crew of the latter.

The *Ann Falcon* with 140 tons of oats grain drifted close past Glashedy on a windless day with a huge swell and later broke up on the Bar. From some of these wrecks crewmen took refuge on Glashedy and there are local tales of a schooner wreck on the island itself. You can read more details of these in Ian Wilson's excellent book *Donegal Shipwrecks*.

Glashedy looks from the shore like the upper half of a fisherman's cap with a bobble on top. At low water the gravelly beach on its south side resembles the peak of the cap. Hundred foot precipices surround the islet, less than 300 yards in diameter. Reefs surround it like the spikes of a hedgehog and hardly make it a practical site for a Gent's Des. Res. but lots of people have taken up temporary abode – men on the run, poteen makers and hermits.

Ringed by the fire of western sunset, Glashedy's black silhouette looks menacing and even more menacing in a winter gale when the waves crest the cliffs. Breaking the silver track of the moon in a shimmering sea it is alluring.

But for all its hazards of approach, Glashedy has had several important functions. Firstly it was a refuge from sea raiders: the Danes in some centuries, Barbary slavers, and O'Flaherty and O'Malley crews from the west in others. Now it is a sanctuary of another sort for geese and for seals, whose calves are born in the caves below. Also a feeding ground for snipe and woodcock in frost when the high ground ashore is too hard for their bills to penetrate.

It is an exciting picnic place for adventurous small boat sailors. There is one bit of shoreline on the southeast corner where you can thread in between half-tide rocks to land. Picnicking is a long standing tradition – a hundred years ago, a benevolent landlord used to let it be known that he was planning a visit with his family so as not to disturb the work of the poteen makers who could arrange not to be stilling that day.

Now we come to the real importance. Making good poteen takes time and concentration. The last thing you want is visits from hard-nosed coastguards or gaugers with nasty threats of seizure and fines. So you work in wildest weather when it would be impossible for a boat to be launched. You have, before that, got all the kit out to the island by currach, launched through surf in moderate weather. Wood and turf for a fire, barley and bottles – treacle or yeast if you can lay hands on any, sugar if you cannot. Then you want a spell of wild gales. It takes say fifteen hours to make the first 'wash' with various esoteric ingredients. For a modest 40 gallons this might involve five boilings of a big iron pot.

Then after a period of 'barming', preferably hidden in pots buried in the earth, the wash is poured into another container which has a tight cap and an aperture at the top

King. The *craic* is good, her beds are comfortable and her breakfasts of Tor-like dimensions.

Opposite it on the sea's edge the homely wooden hut, where the island nurse dispensed loving care, has been replaced by the high pitched blue roof of a Health Centre. I hope it stands up to gales as well as did its predecessor. A big new school caters for some forty children. Dollars as well as Euros have been pouring in at an unprecedented rate to benefit the population which now numbers 175.

Tory is much the same size as Iona in Scotland. Both islands have that heightened vibratory frequency which only comes from centuries of deep faith and battles bravely fought. Both islands have colourful people whose friendship is something to be prized.

The earliest of the islands artists was Jimmy Dixon, a fisherman, farmer and healer who painted for thirty years from 1952 until his death in 1978. In early days he used brown parcel paper as a canvas and a brush made from the hairs of a donkey's tail. The first picture he gave me – now my most prized possession – shows *Caru* blown flat in squall. Jimmy's caption reads:

Mr Wallace Clark passing Tormor, Tory Island in his yacht with a whole gale of S.W. wind and rain with Jill and others on board after leaving Greenport with daybreak about the year 1952. By James Dixon.

Later he and other Tory painters were greatly encouraged by Derek Hill, an Annigoni pupil of international fame, who used the old Lloyds Signal Station on the north cliffs as a workshop. Derek died in 2001, sadly missed by all on Tory; he will be famed forever for his breathtaking landscapes of the north cliffs, which resemble a fortress of the ancient Gods.

Walk out east to see the Wishing Stone on the apex of Balor's Fort. The stone is isolated by a gully from the headland and has a sloping top about two foot square; if you can toss three pebbles in succession to lodge there, and avoid falling over the sheer cliffs on either side while doing so, your wish is bound to come true!

Balor was a disagreeable man, with two eyes in front plus one at the back, a laser that could kill at fifty paces. He condemned people he didn't like to a slow death jammed half way down a hundred foot gully, which ends in the sea. Tory stories place his date from a few years ago in the warship era to a 1000 years B.C. Not a word of a lie! Past and present become one and the same in the delightful Tory way.

The stronghold named after Balor, 300 yards wide by 400 long, is the greatest peninsula fort in Ireland. Guarded on three sides by sheer red precipices and on the fourth by triple ramparts it served for hundreds of years as a refuge. The first recorded raid is by an O'Flaherty sea captain in A.D. 535. In 736 Selbach, Prince of Dalriada captured the

Tor Mor, Tory Island

fort by night and bore off Brude, the Abbot of St. Colmans Abbey. The Vikings raided often. It's not much wonder that the monks, to have security close at hand, built an 80 foot round tower near their church.

The islanders were no slouches when it came to counter-raiding on the mainland. At one stage they established such a reputation for carrying off cattle that the name Tory became synonymous with thief. It is said that is how it came to be used by Whigs as a rudery for their political opponents.

Many monks and abbots have added to Tory's feel of piety but by far the greatest was Columcille. There is hardly a rock without a Columban anecdote. Fifteen hundred years ago he banned rats from the island. In spite of some thirty shipwrecks, no rats have ever reappeared. Not one. Ponder that, Oh, Ye of little faith!

The perils the Tory community has so successfully overcome for centuries will, no doubt, help it to preserve its identity and cohesion in the face of ever closer connections with the mainland. That is perhaps about to become the biggest challenge in three thousand years. But Iona, where Columcille founded his principal monastery, has adapted to a similar challenge and so has Rathlin.

Visit Tory, help it if you can, and wish its inhabitants well.

Inishdooey

We slipped our lines after breakfast on Tory and, driven by a spanking west wind, were in the lee of Inishbeg in less than half an hour.

This uninhabited islet was the scene on 7th Dec 1940 of a most courageous rescue. A Dutch vessel, the *Stolwijk*, had broken down after leaving a convoy in a westerly gale. Judge the conditions by the fact that her destroyer escort lost four men trying to take her in tow before she struck the west end of Inishbeg by night. The Aranmore lifeboat set out at dawn in visibility less than 50 yards and managed to anchor upwind of the wreck where 18 men were clinging for their lives. She fired a rocket line and brought four men off by breeches buoy before the line cut through on a sharp plate on the wreck. The lifeboat crew, stripped of oilskins because they hampered their efforts, with green waves coming waist deep over them had twice more to haul up the anchor, reposition and re-coil the complex lines. The last rocket brought the remaining Dutchmen to safety. The men had been exposed for 22 hours by the time the survivors were landed. The British and Dutch governments later made cash awards as well as gold and silver medals to the crew.

Dramatic caves penetrate the eastern cliffs of Inishdooey. We found dinghy access inshore of Bealadoon Rocks. This was through a narrow gut which led thirty yards up over a fine gravel floor.

Looking over Dooey's Church, Inishdooey to Inishbeg and Tory

Inishdooey

The island's patron is Saint Dubhthach. Don't be put off by a pronunciation problem. His friends called him Dooey, and hence the island's name. He was born about 900 A.D. of royal blood and trained in the discipline of St. Columba.

It was a short walk to Dooey's roofless church on a hill-side at the north end of the island. The beautifully formed eastern window is intact and the vibes of religious fervour remain strong. Several dwellings adjoin and the remains of a stone wall define the monastery ground.

Saint Dooey was very strong on observing the Sabbath. All non-essential activities had to cease but (big deal) if pagans such as Vikings decided to make a call parishioners were allowed to flee. 'Where to?' one might ask. A stand might be made in the doon on the promontory at the southeast end. Some lives may have been saved but it was the Vikings who put an end to worship here.

Well, it wasn't Sunday, so we thought that Dooey's rules would permit the combing of a nearby storm beach. There was lots of flotsam among the boulders including a massive mallet that might have been used to club seals in the Arctic and a gumboot which as Ros remarked might suit a one-legged lady or gentleman for indoor use.

Window at Dooey's Church

30

Inishbòffin

Soon it was time to shift berth and motor across to Boffin. At 3pm the anchor went over the bow with a phosphorescent splash. The water was so clear that we could watch its tooth bite into clean sand twenty feet down. We were in Toberglassan Bay sheltered from the west by a 'secret silver beach' as it was described to Terry by island children and it is indeed hidden from the village or the mainland as it joins the two halves of dumb-bell shaped Inishboffin. For those who love sparkling spring water there is a secret tober, or well, on the eastern shore. It was blessed by Columba and cures diverse ailments, including hangovers. This is a snug anchorage amid harmonic curves with a rare blend of colours from silver sand to flowery vegetation and variegated rocks.

O'Donovan was a Government Surveyor who in 1830 had to decide which place names to put on the first Ordnance maps. He picked Inishboffin, meaning 'Island of the White Cow.' This reference is to *Glas Gevlin*, a lactiferous beast with huge teats that never ran dry. She was stolen just a few years back, so they told us, by Balor, King of Tory, from a mainland blacksmith and hidden for a while on Boffin. But she ate so much grass that no island could satisfy her for long and she had to be moved on.

We rowed south to the beach and walked across sward bright with flowers – Irish eyebright, purple fumitory, kidney vetch – over the rounded top of the island to a row of whitewashed houses facing the mainland. Men were busy building a new hostel, installing septic tanks, and preparing to receive electricity and water from the mainland. But they had plenty of time to talk.

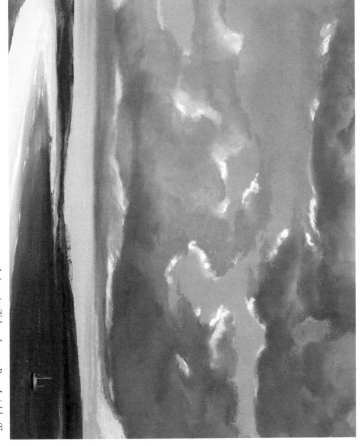

Agivey in Toberglassan Bay, Inishboffin

In years past half the disposable income of a community depended on how the salmon took. It was hard dangerous work – the rougher the night the more fish get into the drift nets. A Boffin boat was cut in half off the Foreland by a steamer a few years back. She didn't stop. The men hung on and tied the two halves together but only the young one survived the night. Another boat was swamped in 1931 in the 'keelie,' that is the sound between Boffin and Dooey. A wave broke clean over the top of her as wind met tide in the narrows. Recently multi-mile filament drift nets have played such havoc with stocks and fish farming has brought prices down so fast that salmon yield is not what it was. So it is as well that Boffin is turning to tourism. But salmon fishing is in the blood and will continue.

While the crew explored, Bee McGonigle gave me a strup-pagh of milk and a scone by her kitchen fire as well as rest from the morning's exertions. When I was first here about 1950 there were 25 families resident in summer. Each had a boat or a share in one. That meant 20 skiffs pulled up on the rocky foreshore facing Muckish, the hump-backed mountain a bit south of the coast.

Skiff or yawl was just the Boffin name for the slim double-ended drontheims built for salmon fishing on Lough Foyle.

Toberglassan Bay with Tory beyond

There are two big days a year in the life of a Donegal fishing port. One is the Blessing of the Boats. This year it was to be a big event with every boat freshly painted and hung with flags and bunting. Crowded with crew and family she would then parade past the priest for benediction. A day of fun combining business and pleasure. The other is the start of the Salmon Fishing season. On our visit this was just two days off and the activity on the foreshore was feverish. Nets being checked for holes, ropes overhauled, floats inflated, oars and hulls painted, engines cranked into life.

Inishboffin

Boffin anchorage is too exposed to leave boats afloat and the 26-foot drontheim was the largest that could be pulled up the rocky foreshore.

Boats fished under sail and their high peaked spritsails were a common sight. Minke whales were numerous enough to be a problem and occasionally upset a boat. Then engines came in and the 'little- bugger- big- bugger' puttering rhythm of slow running paraffin engines echoed across the waters.

By 1970 no more than half a dozen families came out in the summer. Now the numbers are on the up again. Boffin is joined to Donegal by a spit so shallow that at low spring tides carts can trundle across. Some of the neat white houses facing the mainland may once more be filled all the year round.

Out in the Western sea—Oh! how can I tell of them?
Little and wild they be, yet swift is the spell of them:
Swept by the clean sea wind. Oh! the blow and brine of it,
Kissed by the summer sun: Ah! the shimmer and shine of it.

Elisabeth Shane

Inishsirrer

Sailing west from Inishboffin to visit Sirrer in *Agivey* in July 2002 we had an uncomfortable two-hour beat round the Foreland with the tide turning the waves into grey-bearded breakers as it ran against the wind. It was a blessing to turn south and bring the wind abeam and an hour later to get the anchor down into the lee of the island. Then we found the wee pier fractured and the approach made dangerous by broken-off chunks of concrete.

Sirrer is the most northerly and exposed of the Rosses. Its name is probably a variation of sheer meaning outer. Islanders call it Inishsutter, or more often just Sutter. A mile long and narrow, it has grazing on top and rock armoured sides. Today the gables and chimney pots stick up along its spine like the spikes on a crocodile's back. There's lots of turf, so dark and dense as to need little drying. Some hollows grow good rye for cattle feed; others favour corn and potatoes. At the inshore end is a 200 yard wide bay, handy for anchoring on account of its sandy bottom.

My first visit to Sutter was about 1959 in a ten foot currach from Buninver. While I sat on the bare ribs in the stern Corny Haley, tall and lean with muscles rippling along bare forearms and a mouth like a sword cut, knelt on a pad of sacking in the bow. From there he propelled us by drawing the vessel forward at great speed with an oar like a spade. Half way across I noticed my bottom getting wet and looking down saw a tear in the black canvas cover still referred to, from days when it was sealskin, as the 'hide.' Corny undaunted took off a sock and put it the hole. Landing at the island he borrowed smouldering peat from the nearest house and used it to melt some tar to apply a cotton patch; that would be good enough for his night's fishing offshore.

Corny was as good a hand with a pair of oars as a paddle. He won prizes in several All Ireland Currach Championships. Now he showed me the advantages of the ten-foot paddling currach – peculiar to the north Rosses. Working lobster pots near the shore the fisherman facing forward right in the bow can see an underwater rock in time to avoid it. A Sutter currach, with its 5 foot beam, is slim enough to slip between close-set boulders or enter a narrow port in a way that would not be possible for a rowed boat with its spread of oars. It is light enough for one strong man to put it on his back and carry it up a beach or slipway. So it can be launched, according to the wind, off a beach or rock on the lee side of the island.

One house was occupied and Paddy Friel made us welcome there. He told me how the handsome Barnacle Geese stretch out their black necks almost into his door to feed on scraps in spring. But they'd fly off at once to another island if a stranger appeared. Then he talked of old days when there was a resident well-knit community.

"We had all we wanted on the island – spuds, fish, mutton and wool. Tea and sugar came from the Co-op shop a mile up the road from Glashagh beach. In those days you could' a left a currach on the beach when you went shopping. Now the youngsters would have it wrecked before you got back to it".

"Mail was brought out in a currach twice a week rowed by Charlie Gallagher. This place is so beautiful that I'll keep coming back in summer as long as I'm able."

Teague McCullagh, one of the last survivors of those born on Sutter, is a handsome seventy eight year old with deep-

set eyes under curved brows, a hook nose and shock of white hair. His stiff jaw and powerful shoulders tell of strength and determination. With a near perfect memory he looks as if he could pull an oar as well as ever. His grandfather Sean McFadden reared 14 of a family on the island. When Teague was born there were twelve houses occupied all the year round. As boys Teague and his brothers used to fish with lines in the brackish lake at the east end.

"If we caught anything in it we thought we were great men altogether. By the age of twelve I was helping to cut seaweed off the rocks to make kelp for manuring the land. Once or twice starting at five in the morning I rowed a load of it six miles south to reach Annagarry pier at the top of a high tide. There it sold for five shillings. A stone of dulse [edible sea weed] at that time fetched fifteen pennies. It took some gathering. But a stone only had ten pounds in it in those days – I don't know why".

In 1939 Teague was hired out to work for a family on another island; his jobs were footing turf, helping with boats and minding sheep.

"Slave labour it was. Don't write of good old days", he said. "They were bad days – We were often soaked, cold and hungry, and counting the weeks until November. Sometimes your only meal could be some dried seaweed heated up with a few pickles of barley. At the end of eight months I was paid just two pounds."

South-East Inishsirrer

"Getting cattle off Sutter was a tricky job. At a low tide we used to drive them along the rocks towards the Damph. That left about half a mile to swim to Glashagh beach. Two men in a currach could tow three beasts. But if a cow didn't want to swim she was just deadweight and it took another man in a currach to follow and beat an oar at her heels. And donkeys! Nothing'd persuade an ass to swim. They mostly had to be hog-tied and lifted into the currach."

"We kept the half deckers afloat in the salmon season; and when they wern't needed pulled them up on the south side at Cladaghbane. Good shelter but too narrow to anchor in."

"Time o' the War, there was a lot of wreckage—baullks of timber, bales of rubber, bags of flour. One day an island boat found a big barrel out in Tory Sound. It was floating so high they thought it was empty but managed to tow it in. Set on end ashore it was six feet high and made of oak nearly two inches thick. When my father put a hole in it with an auger there was a wild hissing. Everyone thought it was a mine and going to explode so ran like hell. Then they saw brown stuff spraying out and it smelled of whiskey. So we had a hundred and twenty gallons of it! I didn't know much about whiskey in them days. But every house got jugs and buckets full. A lot was hidden and the whole island was drunk for a week. Then the bloody Garda ashore got word of it and came out to get samples. They took lots of samples; then they were ordered to put salt water in the barrel to spoil the lot."

"I'm glad the days of donkeys and horses are over." Teague continued, "It was very sore on them. They were just treated like machines – cruel at times. A donkey might be tethered out on two yards of rope and then made to carry a big load."

There was a famous wreck in February 1832. Teague unfolded a faded press cutting.

SCHOONER LOST AT WEST END OF 'INISIRIR.'
Bravery of Gweedore Men

She struck at night in a northwest gale, and sank almost at once; one man was drowned and the other three were thrown onto the top of a high perpendicular rock.

"I think it must a' been the one we call Toradoo. It's a quarter of a mile east of the north point." said Teague. "In the morning islanders tried to throw them potatoes and coals of fire but it was too far. It seemed impossible to get the survivors off in the wild surf between the island and rock. But another night of exposure would a' killed them. Sutter men were not ones to brag but counted themselves the best of all boatmen in the Rosses. So three currachs were launched, two men in each. They managed to get across in gaps between the waves. The sailors had to jump down the sheer face of the rock. The skipper, weighing 14 stone, nearly wrecked one of the currachs. But all three were got safe ashore. It was like a miracle."

So Inishsirrer has had more than its share of excitement over the years and recognition has been given to the bravery of its people. But it was not enough to save the resident population. By 1943 there were only seven families. If someone became ill it took four men to man a boat and with the young away doing seasonal work in Scotland there were rarely that number available. The school was about to close for lack of children. In the autumn the rest had to leave. In 2002 we scrambled ashore over slippery shifting boulders. Seabirds muddy the pond, where Teague used to fish, but the island is as beautiful and peaceful as ever.

The people of the Rosses islands are a great race — with the natural dignity of folk whose life has been hard and precarious. Their spirit is still evidenced in the remaining houses. Some are roofless; some show a pattern of slater's laths against the sky. One has a ship's deck for a floor, beams and all. Interior walls, peeling in the damp, reveal patches of half a dozen different colour schemes. Most dwellings have a sort of gallery where adults could sleep. Others have box beds, or beds in outshots, with distinctive diamond heads to their posts. Here people lived and loved while gales made the whole atmosphere salt-laden and spray burst over the island to ruin crops.

One cannot have anything but the deepest respect for people who reared families in such conditions.

Inishmeane

'Middle Island' is half a mile in diameter and shaped like an apple with several bites out of it. The biggest bite, on the inshore side, gives some shelter to a stone pier and bouldery beach. Above it a dozen houses cluster on a steep rise. Meane (pronounced to rhyme with can) was abandoned about 1974 but her people have retained their ownership and some still return to live there every summer.

My wife and I first visited Meane in a nine-foot wooden dinghy. We had anchored *Wild Goose* in the shallow water off the pier in the summer of 1958. As we arrived the shop boat was alongside and Messrs Gallagher and Friel were spreading their wares out on the pier. They came round once a week, calling at seven isles. Gumboots mingled with rosary beads and fishhooks were perched on bags of meal, boxes of biscuits supported a bundle of *The Derry Journal*, carrots and plug tobacco sat side by side. An upturned curach acted as a counter for bags of sweets and children's toys. Some shoppers from the fourteen families were looking over the goods in leisurely fashion while others chatted in in turf for the fire, milk the cow, churn butter and help to dry fish. Her husband, she showed us, was making an oilskin by applying layer after layer of boiled linseed oil to an ankle-length cotton smock she had sewn for him. Now it was hanging out in the street to dry like a ghost's haunting sheet.

Bridgie looked so unconsciously happy and fulfilled that her conversation remains clear in my mind almost fifty years on.

Prolonged experience of the beauty of western skies at sunset and glimmering seas at dawn, cultivates within the soul of islanders an awareness of the immense power and mystery of the spiritual world. Nature's wild extravagance and not infrequent cruelty breeds understanding and tolerance. For regularity there is the comforting predictability of twice-daily tides.

Celtic monks came to isolated rocks like the Skelligs for just such experience and to learn the unity of things temporal and eternal, of man and animal. Some of these truths became buried, almost forgotten, in mediaeval western churches. There are signs today of a renewed acceptance.

Fortunately one does not have to be a monk to find such contacts quite quickly on islands today. Below us a currach was coming in and the man in it transferring lobsters into a floating keep-box referred to as a 'hotel'. The mainland

Gaelic on the paved parade which ran between the seawall and four houses facing the sea. Purchases were bartered against wrack, kelp, lambs, eggs or knitwear.

Yachts were rare in those days – we might have been the first one ever to call. A bonny dark-haired woman with bright eyes and red cheeks asked us into her kitchen where scones were baking on a griddle over a turf fire. She'd traded hen eggs for new shoes for her son, so while we sat on creepie stools by the fire he was wriggling his toes inside them and dancing around with delight.

Over her half door Bridgie could see what a Greek poet 1500 years ago recalled as *the innumerable smiles of the waves.* The mile of sea which divides Meane from the mainland is ruffled by winds but sheltered from big breakers except in winter gales. On the far side are two miles of white strand as fine as any in Ireland. Beyond it the scree-covered cone of Errigal soars heavenwards, like a pyramid ten times as high as any in Egypt.

Bridgie had been born on Meane. From the security of island life she looked on the mainland without envy … somewhere to go occasionally for Mass or shopping but live there? Oh No!! Each evening she saw her husband off in his one-man currach to fish for cod and pollock. There were other currachs in company and he had a bottle of Holy Water in the bow so she didn't worry about him too much. Her jobs were to get the children to school, bring

Inishmeane

so close must have made some island men feel weary of the hardships of fishing at times. But the love of island was stronger. It is compounded of many things – individualism, self sufficiency, the pleasure of seeing the dawn rise over water and feeling salt spray on your face, of breathing pure air where children could grow up knowing and being known by every person who lived on the island. The feeling of being part of a community inside boundaries which are finite, not man-made.

It was time to explore. We thanked our fair hostess and walked up a steep stony path between a twin row of two-storey houses. To our right were fields of potatoes and barley. Beyond them was a turbary, cut in neat rectangles, where peats were being set up in footings to dry. Meane is listed as 240 acres but somehow to describe an island by its acres is like rating the Sistine Chapel by its square footage.

Today it feels a well-loved comfortable island of size which allows a day visit to take in most of its features but still leave some secrets for further exploration. Away to our left, cocks crowed around little stone huts on the shore where their mates were dutifully laying and clocking eggs. The road curved ahead over the brow of a hill towards a pair of isolated houses, swanky with tiled roofs instead of the more common thatch. A snipe zigzagged away from our feet. Intriguing to me were several paddling currachs lying 'mouth down'. One with its canvas removed showed the intricate pattern of ribs and stringers which uniquely com-

bine strength, flexibility and lightness. We had a grand walk until it was time to set sail.

Ten years later my ten year old son Milo and I covered the same ground. A white goat came up and butted him playfully, and then he became alarmed when it got its horns under his anorak and threatened to lift him off his feet. We soon disentangled the pair but Inishmeane has been Billy Goat Island to us ever since!

In 2002 Meane seemed lucky to have a rebuilt pier and four beautifully kept houses inhabited in summer. Other houses have roofs intact and are still owned by islanders. No holding, we were told, has been sold outside.

4. Gola and Umfin

Gola

Somewhere I found a list of diseases as yet unclassified by medical science and among these occurred the word 'Islomania' which is described as a rare but by no means unknown affliction of the spirit. There are people, a note adds, who find islands somehow irresistible. The mere knowledge that they are on an island, a little world surrounded by the sea, fills them with an indescribable intoxication.

Lawrence Durrell – Reflections on Marine Venus

Gola lies five miles south off the Bloody Foreland and half a mile off the entrance to Bunbeg. It is shaped like a piece of jigsaw puzzle, a mile north to south and the same between extreme points east to west.

A lugubrious sociological survey, published as a book in 1969, predicted total abandonment inside two years. Instead Gola is now perhaps the best organised of all the Rosses. Three thousand people visited it when a ferry was running from Bunbeg in the year 2000 and in 2002 water and electricity were piped out from the mainland. Comfortable new houses continue to go up. Trails are signposted for

backpackers and climbers find testing pitches on the western cliffs.

Gola is divided from the mainland by a sound four-fathoms deep and half a mile wide. A bigger problem than this trivial distance is a shifting sand bar, almost dry at low water springs, at the entrance to the mainland port of Bunbeg. My wife and I have good reason to remember this. In July 1958, three months before our eldest son was born, we were anchored inside Roaring Rock on the east side of Gola. June is normally an excellent and fearless sailor but when a sudden swell arose and *Wild Goose* started to roll fiercely, she began to feel very sick.

I was in a dilemma, feeling compelled to get her into Bunbeg for shelter but the tide was ebbing. Failing to find the correct way in we could be stranded, bumping on the bar for hours. I shouted to Micky Diver who was passing in his fishing boat and explained the problem.

"I'll get you in," he said without hesitation.

In a twinkling he tied his punt up astern of us and took the tiller while I upped the anchor. Within fifteen minutes

43

we were approaching the bar with breakers on either side of a narrow gap. Confidently he steered us through with a foot to spare under our iron keel. Then we were into calm water, with half a mile of twisting channel to negotiate to the deep-water anchorage off The Bluff.

Half an hour later it would have been too shallow. We've had help from Donegal fishermen on lots of occasions but none more timely than that. It was typical of the kindness of Gola to a stranger.

With the anchor down Micky accepted a dram.

"I suppose I might have found the way on my own," I queried, but he shook his head.

"Never play with the sea, Mr Clark." He had a nice way of drinking in small gulps as he relaxed in the cockpit and told us of the fishing cycle. It was salmon in early summer – mostly at night with the constant worry about the net fouling rocks as the tide did its best to twist it into a figure of eight – potting for crabs and lobsters after that, herring in the autumn, cod in January, pollock and flatties at any time.

"That's all the water we have to make our living in winter", he explained pointing to the semi-sheltered bay between Gola and Inishmeane.

Next morning, Sunday, we watched a procession of

crowded boats pass us on their way to Mass. An hour later they passed us going back. A sore temptation it must have been to the youngsters to stay ashore for the spurious delight of the town. This weekly glimpse of the mainland must have been quite a factor in making people decide to live ashore.

Mobility of dwelling was common in the Rosses. The practice of 'booleying' or summer grazing on mountain pasture meant that many families had access to three houses, one each on mainland, an island and mountain slopes.

Later we explored Gola and were impressed by the many large boulders left by shrinking glaciers at the end of the last Ice Age some 10,000 years ago. Gola has a pier and slipway on each side, one reason, perhaps, why it was noted as the community which fished most. There was always access to sheltered water. There are several little coves where you can lie according to wind direction.

One 15th August a couple of years later, June and I were anchored in one called Mweelmore, a semi-circular bay surrounded by red rock cliffs. Still not overlooked by houses it reminded us of calanques where we had holed up in southern France.

Most of the inhabitants, it seemed, came to watch us that day – men in blue suits and girls in print dresses. Then I realised it was Saturday, the Feast of the Assumption and work was forbidden. We hoisted the sails and got ready

On Gola looking towards Errigal on the mainland

to beat out against a light southerly breeze. Somehow we missed stays and seemed sure of a grounding on the rocky foreshore. The islanders saw just what was about to happen and half a dozen sprinted down to push us off. *Wild Goose* with her usual good luck picked up a wee back wind off the cliffs, got her head round and just sailed clear. There was friendly cheer from the shore.

Nesting Cormorants

The Congested District Board bought out Gola from the Hill family and did a power of good after 1892. Bridges, dams, barns and piers were among the items subsidised and the name of the Board often became attached. 'Congested' barns are common on Gola, about 25 feet square with an upper story suitable for air-drying grain, assisted by the heat rising from animals stabled below.

Another visit was in the 16-oar galley *Aileach* in May 1991. We pushed her nose up on the beach just inside the south point and had a picnic lunch. There was an air of decay about the island with sheep droppings and occasional carcases in many doorless houses. I don't recollect any inhab-

ited houses but it must have been soon after this that the demand began for holiday homes on islands.

Aileach was a replica Highland Galley following the route that Somerled took about 1166 on his way back to Scotland to start a long war against the Vikings. Some island men joined him and helped win victories which made him Lord of the Isles. The tradition holds. In 1912 there were two Gola men as crew in the *Asgard* when she ran in rifles to arm the Irish Volunteers. Their names are commemorated on a pillar on top of the island.

Gola has retained its insular pride and is a lovely active place to visit.

Umfin

Umfin offers all the excitements of a desert isle. It is beautiful, humpbacked, difficult to land on and rarely visited.

A third of a mile long it is the biggest of a cluster of chunky red sisters which lie close off the north tip of Gola. An emerald cap of grass, much more vivid than the swards of its neighbours, is its distinguishing mark. The name is pronounced Umfin, with emphasis on the first syllable. Tornacolpagh, Tornascarden, Tororragaum and Torbane are the poetic names of the rest of the group.

Their common feature is near vertical sides of granite tinged with iron ore. This mix produces the pleasing shades of red from which the Bloody Foreland gets its name.

The cliffs are scratched as if some giant sea cat had stropped its claws up and down, then sideways. The effect is a singular reticulation of dark lines on the pink and ochre background. A huge cat's paw has gone right through in places to make tunnels from one side of an isle to the other – or vertically to make holes in a cave roof. Such apertures become, in a western gale, blowholes through which great gouts of white spray leap skywards to the accompaniment of booms like gunfire.

On a fine day the yellow tide foam which accumulates in patches in the island's lee is blown like giant soapsuds in picturesque fashion round the crags.

The west-facing cave on Tororragaum has vertical sides and a flat roof, looking like the portal in the Valley of the Kings but the meaning of its name – head of the pollock – proves once again that Irish place names are best un-translated.

Between Umfin itself and Tornacolpagh is a banana-shaped harbour which dries at low water. To shallow draft craft of the right shape to lie aground, it offers shelter from swell and cover from view. From it with a strong enough crew to launch the vessel, an exit could be made at either end, at any time, to take flight or plunder a passing ship.

The sand showing at low water draws the eye in and gives relief from the ironbound sides. It is an idyllic place for a picnic. On that beach fifty years ago were found some blue glass beads analysed as lapis lazuli from Tyre. Sit down and trickle the sand through your fingers. Those million year old grains can stimulate the imagination.

Off Umfin, almost three thousand years ago, Phlebas the Phoenician (the one James Elroy Flecker wrote about) may have furled his sail and conned his shapely beaked galley in under oars. His spade-bearded crewmen were ready to trade Syrian wine, silks and jewellery for slaves or Irish gold. His was by far the earliest voyage by incomers to the west coast for which there is even a crumb of evidence. A thousand years after him Vikings would have found this an ideal base in which to hide their long ships, plan raids, careen and carouse.

Much more recently came the smugglers who rigged sheer legs and purchases to haul a twelve pounder cannon and barrels of powder onto Gun Rock. This is the buttress which shelters the one fathom anchorage at the south end of the gut. Some sea captain must have thought its privacy well worth protecting.

Lord George Hill acquired Umfin about 1850 when he bought most of Gweedore parish and dipped deep into his pocket to make substantial improvements for his thousands of tenants. Much of his holdings have now been sold but his direct descendants retain Umfin, the *isola bella* of the Rosses.

Three houses were marked on the west side in 1860, when the first detailed chart was made, but no one now knows who lived there. Shepherds, perhaps, in summer who looked after calves on Colpagh and sheep on the main island and snared rabbits and geese in their spare time. Human inhabitants had long gone when I first landed there in 1955 but the bunnies abounded.

Umfin, now in splendid isolation, is a place of ancient memories and elfin beauty, with plenty to set your imagination astir.

The Tororragaun blowhole off Umfin

Owey

'Full many a gem of purest ray serene
The dark unfathomed caves of ocean bear.'

Thomas Gray

Agivey got under way at high water and sailed south from Gola with a fair tide. Inishshinney lay inshore of us blocking the mouth of Gweedore Harbour. It once had two families but, that day, was inhabited only by a couple of the jack donkeys after which it is named. Lacking female company they looked frustrated.

We passed the reefs of Deadman's and Horse Rocks which guard the east side of Inishfree Lower, the Heather Isle. It provided home for a family up until about 1970.

Owey lies close off Cruit Island. At sea level its silhouette is like a crocodile. From an aeroplane you can see that it is square with sides about three quarters of a mile long. Hundred foot cliffs sheer all round except for some boulders on the south. The peak at the west rises 350 feet and a road runs up the centre valley straight as a gun barrel from the village to a lake above the western cliffs.

A couple of attempts failed to get the anchor to hold. We were wondering where to try next when an island boat came alongside. She was driven by outboard, and fishing rods stuck out from her stern.

'You'd be better west of the burn. The one that runs down through the village', said Neil Gallagher, her round-faced, genial skipper. 'It's all rocks and wrack here'.

He then towed us to the right spot, gave us a present of several small turbot and a lift in to the quay. This is a shelf on the north side of an unforgettable gut, a hundred yards long and scarcely more than a boat length wide. It is handy for paddling currachs which can easily haul out on the sandy beach at its head. Wooden boats could be dragged up a concrete slip and sheltered from gales in an enclosure of granite boulders at the top. The cost in labour was immense for there were no horses to share the load. So the salmon boats were kept afloat at Kincashla inside lovely Cruit Island.

The Oweyaghs commuted by paddling currach and Neil gave hair-raising accounts of days when the swell was breaking clean across the sound. Young men could get over to

Cruit by careful timing, 'paddling like hell' to make a five minute passage between one breaker and the next!!

"That's the way we went to fish or to Mass in Kincashla".

"Come up to my house later on," said our most kindly host as he went off to resume his fishing. He'd been born on the island, spent quite a long time working in Scotland and now winters near Dungloe, returning to Owey each summer.

His welcome recalled an earlier visit to Gola in *Caru*. 'Crikky' Gallaher came on board from his currach. He hunkered into the cabin – it wasn't high enough to stand up in – and downed a half 'un. Then he patted his ample tum, looked round the varnished cabin and remarked, 'She's a palace, just a wee palace!' I suppose she was, compared to his currach. *Caru* loved the compliment but didn't seem so palatial at night when it was my turn to sleep on the cabin floor. We were four up with only three bunks.

We clambered up steep steps to explore. Owey is properly pronounced oooey, as in zoo. Beneath the upper lake, Neill told us, is a subterranean one accessible only from steps cut in the seaward cliffs. We didn't have time or gear to explore it just then but I intend to go back and try.

On the north west point a shelf near the top is known as the Giant's Seat. An old guidebook refers to a Giant's Grave but Neil says it is just a *pishogue*, invented to match the seat.

Real enough are the caves measureless to man, still not fully explored, that slice and penetrate Owey. You can see an array of their red mouths, tunnels and canyons on the northeast side. They are adorned with red pinnacles, scored by black crevices and are the refuge of birds and mammals. Exploring the outer parts in a small boat in calm weather is exciting. The walls echo the sucking of the swell, the cooing of rock pigeons, the whirr as they take to the wing and the plops as shags drop heavily into the water. These caves are more entrancing by far than the Blue Grotto on Capri.

Seals love wet caves, so Owey has plenty – clever ones too who have learned how to unlatch a lobster pot and feast on the contents. The McDonagh Papers (Donegal Historical Society Yearbook) record that in the 19th Century Owenaghs killed and ate many seals, salted them for winter and preferred seal meat to any other. Their shoes and trousers were sealskin and their currachs were covered in the same odiferous material.

Lobsters were pulled with hooks from crevices in the rocks and weights ran five to thirteen pounds. Scallops, obtained by women wading near naked at low water, weighed from two to four pounds each! Weights which seem almost incredible against today's paltry results of over-fishing.

The necessities needed from the shore were *'baccy and spirits of which both sexes are excessively fond,'* McDonagh continues. *'Women knitted socks to sell but never wore them. They were*

52

Ouey Harbour

Owey Caves

nervous of the mainland and went to market only in groups'.

Owey's most famous product was liqueur poteen, the best on the coast. I once tasted some Old Owey in the house of a former Minister of Lands and Justice. It was as smooth as Islay Laphroig whiskey. Much of the island's turf was used to make poteen leaving areas of bare scree on the west but there still seems to be a fair bit of grazing.

Funerals were spectacular. The corpse, wrapped in a coarse woollen robe was placed in a currach with legs hanging over the stern and a fiddler for company. Then the currach led a procession across some ten miles of open sea to Aranmore for burial. The priest followed in the next currach. Others, up to sixty in number, containing family and friends fell in astern, rowing in time to the fiddler music. Clay pipes were smoked, to be broken later and dropped into the grave. The water-borne cortege practice took a knock in later years when nine mourners were drowned en route from Aran to Templecrone.

54

Brigid, with fine red hair and a figure to turn any gentleman's head, emerged from her cottage and showed us round the village. It consists of two rows split by the stream which runs in a deep gully, providing water for drinking and washing. Peculiarities of the houses were pairs of bedrooms sheeted off at the end of the living room, a development from the box beds of earlier days. A pair of leaning masts were relics of the radio telephone of the fifties. Now there is talk of mains electricity and water being brought out soon.

Owey residents migrated to work in Scotland and America. Eleven served in the US army in W.W.I. This migration habit helped the Rosses to come through the 19th Century famines better than Connemara islands which had no such overseas source of income.

Later as we got back from a walk along the cliffs, Brigid and other capricious ladies invited us to join them bathing in the sandy pool at the head of the harbour. It looked most tempting but it was time for us to emigrate too – on a non-stop voyage of six miles to Burtonport where we were expected for a meal at the Lobster Bar.

Sailing south we could see a foursome of golfers starring a round on the sporting Cruit Island course. Confusingly its name is pronounced Critch, and it is not an island. Three miles long and in places barely half a mile wide its many hillocks yield entrancing views of sea and rocks on either hand.

Approaching Aranmore from the north is a little unnerving. Twenty buoys and beacons demand the attention of the navigator, so many in fact that there are hardly any left for the whole of the rest of the west! But it's not so hard if you have on board the only two things in the world you can trust – a tried friend and a British Admiralty Chart. Have one on your knee, the chart, not the chum. If possible carry Number 1879, the old fathom black and white one. It shows much better detail than the modern coloured metre, Number 1883.

From two miles or more off you make sure to identify Bally Rock ('Ballagh' on the chart). Its 24-foot fat white conical beacon is easy to pick out, and nothing else is remotely like it in the area. Leave it to port and steer south to clear the west side of Eighter Island by a quarter of a mile (to avoid Dirry Rock). From there turn southeast and follow along the eastern shore of the North Channel, made easy by leading lights and beacons which guide the car ferry to Burtonport.

As we passed the red Carrickatine Perch we sighted to port a rocky creek that seemed to go in a long way. Half hidden within it was a cottage and a small quay. 'Let's have a look', said Ros. So we anchored and scrambled into the alloy dinghy, a new acquisition which the crew had just named the *Wallygator*.

Eighter Island

Eighter looks on the chart like a lobster claw projecting northwest, with Illanagal to which it is joined at low water forming the right nipper. On a first visit, yonks ago, we had landed on sticky ooze at the head of the gut. Hens and ducks wandered all over the foreshore where currachs and half-deckers were pulled up.

Mrs Frank O'Donnell invited us into her cottage where a cricket chirped on the hearth. Tea for us was roasted dry in the pot hung from a crane over the turf fire. It seemed a long time until it could be wet. The result was strong enough *'to trot a mouse on and keep a body going all day'*. This lady I afterwards found was referred to as 'The Weekend Bride'. Her husband Frank visited her at intervals from Burtonpart.

In 2002 we had two piers to choose from and found that five cottages had, with minimum external alteration,

Razorbills

become holiday houses. Families who cared for the island and loved it as much as had any previous generation occupied all.

It was a privilege, in Richard's company, to wander over short-cropped turf and round bumpy wee hills. They were often topped with huge boulders as if a giant had left off in the middle of a game of skittles. Now there's a pitch and putt golf course for humans instead. We were shown rare plants in sheltered corners. Orchids, milkwort, wild mint with a sharp taste, yellow rattle and water lilies.

There is a choice of little bays to give shelter in any wind with beaches where you could skinny-dip in privacy. It might have been the place where Masefield wrote

'Coves clean bottomed where we saw
The brown red-spotted plaice
go skimming six feet down.'

The cheerful *'chilloop'* of choughs came over on the breeze and we saw them poking their long red bills into cowpats.

"They're choosey feeders and prefer the grubs which feed in firm manure". Richard pointed out. "Ones that don't occur in drizzly droppings elsewhere".

There is an erosion problem and fences must keep cattle back from beaches to allow marram grass to develop strong

Ballagh Rock Beacon from Eighter

roots. We sat down on the grass with Tom Halifax the artist and his house party to enjoy cans of beer. He next guided us over the bridge to have a bathe in the lake on Inishcoo.

Thank you, Eighteraghs. You gave us a lovely day on your very special private island. You've disproved the cynical French saying that *An island gives pleasure twice in your life, once when you buy it and once when you sell it.'*

It was time to sail on down the channel. Directions to the helmswoman were simple. Leave Goat, Duck and Rutland islands to your right. Inishcoo and Edernish to your left.

Just south of Edernish a mile long open lagoon burst upon our view. Half a mile east across it loomed the ragged masts off Burtonport pier and its marina. Yes, marina! It was all happening in the Year of Our Lord 2003 . The fifty-foot fishing boats and their crews were moving south to Killybegs from where million pound ships pursue huge shoals of fish from Africa to Norway. So the inner Rosses are left for a few lobster-potters and a lot of island lovers and yachties.

According to researchers it was from hereabouts in 550 A.D. that St. Brendan took departure for America. Tim Severin, with whom I sailed partway in his leather-covered currach, would have called here but a gale forced him almost a hundred miles offshore. His *Brendan* departed

Donegal from Ballywhoriskey and got to America a year later.

That association is a reminder that going to sea is man's oldest temptation. The great adventure of Brendan in which religious fervour, the desire for knowledge and the love of challenge were inextricably mixed still fascinates today. The sea has now acquired a wider dimension of pleasure, ecology and sport. Burtonport in allowing tourism to replace commercial fishing is right in line with the trend.

6. Aranmore, Inishkeeragh and Rutland

Aranmore

The inhabitants are highly intelligent and though unedu-cated wonderfully well up in history with a strong belief in ghosts and fairies.

Edward McCarron, Lightkeeper 1870

'There's an island up north so big that you could meet people you didn't know on it'. These words came in tones of wonder from a young islander on Inishkea when we were on a voyage round Ireland back in 1955.

They could only have been referring to Aranmore and even today they still underline its distinguishing feature – SIZE. If you like islands with convivial hotels, pubs and restaurants, connected by car ferry on a sheltered route to the mainland and a lifeboat station, then Aranmore will be your favourite of all the Rosses.

It has plenty of room out west to give that feeling of peaceful solitude that is the most important part of island charm. To judge by the rate at which new houses are going up it remains top of the pops.

On our first ever visit, in 1956, we anchored *Caru* a bit south of Calf Island after an overnight sail and landed on what the chart labelled 'Young Mick's Strand'. No signs of the youthful owner but the chart was made about 1880 so perhaps he slept with his fathers. Not knowing any better we scrambled up a steep bank, forced our way through a fuchsia hedge, climbed over a brambly stone wall and so to the hotel. There we had a splendid Ulster Fry. It was a weekend trip and next day we sailed sixty miles home. Oh, for the energy of youth!

My 1961 memory is of excited islanders in O'Donnells pub in the 'Port', as Burtonport is locally known. In the middle stood the burly figure of Barry who had piloted the mail boat from the Island in the teeth of a never before experienced storm. This was Hurricane Hazel which, with gusts over 110mph, did more damage to Donegal in a day than any other that century.

"You're a great man now , Barry", said one passenger. "You've saved all our lives this day", as he handed over a half un of whiskey and pint of porter.

The great man modestly gave the credit elsewhere.

"Now the only thing I did was pray to St. Peter. But I wasn't sure if it'd be any good in Irish. They say he speaks

English.

"But maybe you got round him better in Irish." said another voice.

"Didn't I just? Sure he took the tiller out of my hand." said Barty as the pint disappeared in one vast gulp. The walls of the old building were shaking in the gusts by now and as the glasses filled the talk became general.

"The crops is arl rooned; kilt by the spray," a girl with welling eyes told me. Jubilation at being safe ashore kept the party going none the less. "One for you, Mr Stranger?" and I was, willy-nilly, included in the round. Three more followed before I could even get my hand in my pocket.

Aranmore is triangular and rises 700 feet to the rounded peak of Cluidaniller. Its population is quoted as about 750 souls. The hill shelters Aran and the isles inshore from the prevailing wind, the bitterest enemy of island farmers. An hour's walk from the ferry quay will take you to the lighthouse at Rinrawros on the northwest point.

There, while inhaling pure ozone, you can admire the Small Giant, a stack of a mere 160 feet. The priapic Big Giant (362 feet) dwarfs it.

Aranmore Light

This coast is dramatic in any light but best admired at night when picked out by the intermitent beams of the great lantern, while the roar of waves below creates a *Son et Lumiere* of a grandeur no theatre could match.

Away out west is Tír Nan Og, the Land of the Ever Young, where good islanders go when they die. It has been sighted and described by sober observers on a couple of occasions not so long ago.

Walking on south you cross great green glens sweeping down to the sea. Random black eyebrows scar them where turf has been cut. At the southwest corner lies hump-backed Green Island, a bird sanctuary where the tourist map marks the wreck of a copper ship.

"How do they know it was carrying copper?" I later asked a fisherman.

"That's easy. The lobsters from round there all come up bright green!" was the reply.

Going on widdershins or anti-clockwise for another hour or two you can reach a perfect staging point at the Atlantic Bar. Sit there, outside if its fine, and overlook a harbour 200 feet below where wooden boats bob around on moorings, Brittany fashion, in a horseshoe natural harbour. While we drank big black pints and munched crab sandwiches, an inflatable came roaring in from the west. They mustn't have known much about Aranmore for they acted as if they thought closing time was near (it never is!) and sprinted up the hill still wearing life jackets.

"Relax, men," said mine host as he served them. "Even the highest tides don't come up this far."

We had a call to pay. It was on Mrs Mary Gallagher some of whose family live near us in County Derry.

"Which one?" was the reply when I asked about her house.

"There are six Mary Gallaghers on the island. Each have nicknames to help the postman."

Her elegant bungalow was close-by with picture windows looking over a trim lawn and a magnificent view south to Glen head in the ineffable Donegal blue of Slieve Tooey. In the foreground Inishkeeragh (Sheep Island), where Mary was born, looked as if it had just come up to breathe.

She told us bits of history. There are traces of Mesolithic dwellings. Smart men, those Flintstones, for Aran is the most fertile of all the Rosses. By 1300 A.D. continental fishing boats came to get permission to work the waters from The O'Donnell, King of Fish. By 1460 there are records of traders bringing wine from Brittany and Spain to meet the thirst of Turlough of the Wine, Lord of Tyrconnel. A horrific attack came in 1680. A Captain Conyngham had ejected MacSweeney of the Battle Axes, a doughty and honourable warrior, from Doe Castle on Sheephaven.

Conyngham was fond of making cattle raids from there. When the islanders saw his galleys arriving many hid in a cave at the south end. After seven days while all the sheep, cattle, liquor and nubile ladies on the island had been

rounded up an old woman peeped out of the cave. She was spotted and all 67 of those hidden were slaughtered. Uamhaigh na Sceilp (the cave of murders) is still pointed out on the shore by St. Crones Church.

Justice was later done when Sheamus Cronne, owner of a gun known as The Mhor, shot Conyngham. His friend Aodh O'Donnell a famed Aran warrior then assisted him to wipe out the escort. The last of these were killed at Illaunn na Gonrach ('Island of Coffins') on Cruit Strand. Perhaps the deaths were salutary, for later members of the Conyngham family seem to have been less hard on tenants.

Edward McCarron, who was a light keeper from 1870 until 1872 before going to Inishtrahull, gives some intimate glimpses of island life in his memoirs entitled *Life in Donegal*. He describes watching islanders at Sunday open air Mass. Two men were working at a boat nearby and began to exchange blows. Half the congregation joined one and half the other. The herring left the area and it was assumed that this fracas was the cause.

The owner at this time was John Charley of Belfast. He had bought Aranmore for £200 in 1848 at a time when Conyngham was anxious to be clear following a critical article in The Times. Charley was only 23 and had been active getting aid during the Potato Famine. He now organised free passages to America for those willing to go, but his motives for this have been questioned. Intended benevolence

The Inner Rosses from Aranmore

Inishkeeragh

This is a flat appendage 600 yards off the south side of Aranmore. From sea level it looks like a row of roofless houses sticking out of the water, so low is the land. The ground is nowhere more than eleven feet high and the spray sweeps right across. Twice in the early 20th Century, when an exceptionally high tide coincided with bad gales, the islanders had to take refuge in the two houses that had lofts. They spent hours in terror, fearing the overloaded floors should collapse.

As a visitor Phil Dinsmore recalls she would be given a boiled egg in each house she called on. Hens were running all around the houses and into the bird marsh at the back. In 2003 the seawall on the north east side in front of the houses is collapsing. It looks as if it would have been better at the rear to provide some shelter from prevailing gales. The old pier, abreast the middle of the houses, has disintegrated but a yacht could anchor as

Gulls at Inishkeeragh

64

by island lairds often turns sour. McCarron later found Charley to be genial and sympathetic but over ready to raise the rent. He built Glen House (now the Hotel) and lived there until his death in 1878. His widow a Donegal girl sold out to the Congested Districts Board in 1889. The light on Charley Point perpetuates the family name.

In the Second World War there was much gallantry. Most famous were rescues by the RNLI Lifeboat, the one described above at Inishbeg and another of a ship's boat plucked from certain death during a westerly gale on the north rocks of Aranmore. For these services gold RNLI and Dutch medals were awarded and are to be found in the lifeboat building. A lightkeeper's wife up at night tending a sick child spotted a crew of Norwegians, some severely steam-scalded, off the rocks on the west. They were hauled to safety up the cliffs. A timber-laden freighter, disabled by bombs, was boarded and guided into Boylagh Bay. The modern Lifeboat now on station continues to save many lives.

Aranmore is a perfect size for island-loving visitors in that you can reach any part of it in the course of a leisurely morning's walk. It is large enough to offer further scope for exploration but small enough for the visitor to take away the impression of an entity, not just a series of places visited.

we have done in nine feet of water off the south east end and land on shingle.

But be careful! A Sea Serpent, with a horse-like bearded head the size of a door on top of a long neck, was sighted by Mary Herdman, of the Edernish family, and fishermen accompanying her hereabouts in 1880. Her nephew sighted it next day scraping its scales against a rock and getting ready to attack a boat. Then it dived and was seen no more.

There were squabbles over rent and land holdings but, for all that, Keeragh was a much-loved island and people still go back for re-unions. Inishkeeragh is another monument to human perseverance and hardihood. I would not be surprised to hear of people starting to recreate holiday houses there.

Rutland

Rutland is a sandy island nestling under the lee of Aranmore. It is big as the inner Rosses go, a mile long by half a mile wide. The western edge is beach. Most of the interior consists of dunes where donkeys used to run wild but is now a garden of wild flowers like Grass of Parnassus. The population lives at the northeast where rocks outcrop and houses face Inishcoo and Edernish across sixty yards of restless tides.

In the morning a yellow sea kayak paddled by Laird Dinsmore came alongside us at Burtonport pier with a message from his father offering a lift to the island. Soon we were piling into Frank's 50 horsepower skimmer. He never travels at less than 25 knots, often more, and his boat can be recognised at once by the pair of black dachshunds staring eagerly over the bow. He handles it as if in an Olympic slalom, dodging ferries, fishing boats, buoys and beacons with consummate skill.

Frank's house, above a stepped pier, is the most northerly on Rutland. From it he scans new arrivals in a fatherly way and checks their national flags and burgees. Smart yacht skippers dip their ensign in salute as they pass and perhaps qualify for a dram when the sun gets over the yardarm.

South of Frank's house is a handsome granite Customs House and store, overlooking an inlet known as the Black

Hole. South again are twin rows of houses facing each other at right angles to the shoreline and known as Duck Street. Just past them is Laird's fine house, balconied to see over a green-topped islet. Like his father's it originated in a fisherman's cottage.

Plenty of history attaches to Rutland. Early references tell of rape and pillage in 1543 by Connaught men. Fame came suddenly in the late 18th Century. It was all to do with herring. Herring feed in huge shoals in mid-ocean. A few weeks each year are spent inshore to spawn. For this job, like us humans, they prefer a bed. In 1780 they started to get on with it in between the myriad Donegal islands. At dusk the fish that stuffed the sounds and bays would rise to the surface. This is when they could be netted by the ton, foul-hooked or caught on a bare hook.

Getting into the sound, deeply laden under sail, was only possible in certain winds. Pulling boats were ready, for a fee, to tow them alongside to discharge and out again to where the herring were.

In 1784 five hundred schooners, luggers, wherries and cutters were engaged in netting herring. At the same game were a thousand open boats – lake cots and coracles from Lough Erne, drontheims from Portrush, currachs from the islands, glotioges and hookers from Galway – anything that would float and 33,000 barrels were landed at Rutland.

Other ships made money by bringing salt for curing, barrel staves and wicker baskets. The quays were cheerful with the chatter of scores of girls gutting the 'silver darlings' and the shouts of curers bidding against one another for so many cran (37 gallons or about 750 fish). The cliffs rang with the blows of cooper's hammers. Eight hundred people lived on Rutland mostly in sod huts that could be put up in few hours. The rumble of barrels passing over stone and clamour of gulls feeding on stranded fish added to a delightful bustle of plenty. The rocks are sheer enough in many places for drifters to be tied alongside and there they lay four and five thick waiting to discharge. Island public houses and shebeens did a 24 hour trade; local profits were estimated at £40,000 per annum. It seemed that The Golden Age had dawned. Fishermen wore silver buckles on their shoes.

The Proprietor of the day, William Conyngham (1733 –96) nephew of the Marquis, spent £20,000 of his own money and a similar sum from parliament in improving the quays and curing houses and making road links for export. In return for some public appointment he changed the name of the island from Inishmacdurn to that of The Duke of Rutland, the Lord-Lieutenant of the day. Being the more easily pronounceable, the new name stuck.

A couple of years later Traweenagh ('tryeenagh') Bay, three miles south, was reported jammed solid with fish. Fighting broke out over who could put a net across the narrow mouth and get real bulk. 'Any blood in the bay' said the

The Union Store, Rutland

superstitious 'and the herring will disappear.' And so they did.

By 1793 the best was over. Herring came back but never reached the bonanza of the eighties. Although Rutland, holding the Post Office and Coastguard Station, was the administrative centre of the Rosses for some 200 years, drifting sand covered the fortified bawn built by Scottish settlers about 1620. In the 19th Century sand ate up a row of dwelling and boathouses as well. From the ferry you can see their buried gables a few yards south of Tomishaun, the most northerly point of the island.

Near here too is the ridge of rock where James Napper Tandy landed from the French brig *Anacreon* on 16th September 1798. He had been a General of Artillery in the Irish Volunteers. On departure from Brest Napper claimed, "I have only to set foot on the Irish coast for thousands of men to rise and join me.' Sadly for him the news came with the mail (which he intercepted at pistol point) that the French General Humbert had already surrendered. The unfortunate locals who had risen to join him were either executed, in prison or on the run. There was nothing that *Anacreon's* contingent of 80 men, or the thousand muskets she carried, could achieve on their own. So, after spending a nostalgic evening with his friend the Postmaster, Napper was carried insensible back on board.

One feels sympathy for Napper. He lacked the luck that is essential to any commander. If he had arrived earlier Rutland might have become a famous bridgehead for further French landings, diverted the troops that defeated Humbert and we'd all be speaking French now.

Napper had more ill luck on the way back. He was betrayed, handed over to British authorities and condemned to death in Dublin. But, at last, he drew such wide sympathy as to attract a Royal Pardon.

In the 1850s Rutland remained important and had a shebeen for passing sailors and a Union Store. Decline came in the 20th Century when steam trawlers began to work off the coast and a channel across the sands was dredged to Burtonport. There, catches could be landed more economically so Rutland lost out but kept up its population. In 1960 there were still twenty island families and thirty children at school. Gradually, folk moved to the mainland.

Rutland is a-buzz in summer once more with half a dozen families – a trend started many years ago by the Dinsmores and others who understand boats and the needs of islands. They have converted fishermen's cottages tastefully into second homes. Islands need incomers who can get the feel of the place and bring in some additional funding. That seems to be happening in the right way for Rutland.

7. Lahan, Edernish and Inishcoo

The only really proper way to get to places is in a sailing yacht by your own efforts.

Erskine Childers, 1902

Agivey was now in a sheltered area of short distances and definite places. From quiet anchorages we would be able to identify, at our leisure, the bold anfractuous rocks to avoid and low beach-ringed islets to visit.

Off Burtonport is a water world that comes socially alive in July and August when holiday homes are manned and there are parties every night, but it is just as enjoyable in winter when you have, for company, wind blown skeins of seafowl and the dawn cry of the curlew.

Having negotiated the narrows between Rutland and Edernish a bit before high water, we decided to follow the dredged channel east and tie up alongside the pier at Burtonport for bunkers and a meal at the Lobster Bar.

That evening, on our way a mile north to Lahan Island, a vast dramatic sunset over Eighter showed the black silhouette of Aran ringed in fire.

Lahan

Lahan means 'broad' because it presents its 500-yard rocky flank to the northwest swell in contrast to the spearhead points of other inshore islands. It lies close to the mainland just south of Castle Port. The castle, which gives this sandy cove its name, is now just a few stones visible at low water but Lahan itself is a circular natural strong point. Satellite rocks lie all round and a steep wee peninsula sticks out east.

A snug south-facing hollow, sheltered by an eighty foot hill, contains a solitary cottage – most inviting with its blue door and tiny windows. It might have been made as a hideaway for honeymooners with heather at the door and a distant view of Errigal. In fact Barbara Buchanan, then resident in Tyrone, rebuilt it with the islands pink granite some fifty years ago. Ruins, smothered in bracken, tell of four other cottages. Barbara is remembered as 'the wee Canadian' who was given to currach racing round the island with James 'Owey' Gallagher who had built a pair. One of these accompanied her when she returned to her homeland about 1980. So if you see a ten foot currach shooting rapids on the Mackenzie River you'll know where it came from!

Edernish

What is cosier than the shore
Of a lake turned inside out?
How can all these other people
Dare to be about?

W.H. Auden

Richard and Shirley Scot whose hospitality we have often enjoyed are owners of long standing. Their spuds, manured with kelp, are as epicurean as the winkles, mussels, and cockles to be picked off the rocks or shrimps netted under the attaching seaweed.

Two systems of transport are available to commuters: on foot across level sand at low water or by dinghy at other times to a fine granite pier that was erected long ago, seemingly just for Lahan. But they forgot to put a road to it. Perhaps it was part of the same contract for a village ten miles inland whose inhabitants got jealous, in Balfour days, of money and jobs going to seasiders. So they applied for a pier. Hurriedly approved, it was built in the midst of a ploughed field. I was told where, ages ago, but perhaps like much else in Ireland, that is best forgotten.

Lacking electricity and running water the cottage can hardly be labelled 'all mod cons'. To stay there is more an education in camping than an experience of *grande luxe* but I don't know of a more idyllic islet for private holidays or *recherché* barbecues.

The next morning I was woken early by something whizzing low over our masthead. It happened a second time and I was about to take cover when I realised that rocks were being blasted for the new Burtonport Marina.

Sleep was impossible so I pulled across the flats in the *Wallygator* (our dinghy) to see how Edernish had changed. Crabs scuttled across the clean sand under the keel as I rowed across.

The islet, as its name '*Idir Inish* – Middle Island' implies, stands at the centre point of the inner Rosses. So its cream-coloured three storey wooden house of pleasing proportions is widely visible and could be described as the most striking building in the area. Rolf, the German owner, was not at home but I took the liberty of landing at the elaborate boat storage arrangements he has built at the south end – a steel pier, big slip, electric winch and well equipped workshop.

The Herdman family, linen manufacturers like my own, erected the frame house of Swedish pine in 1904. It

70

appeared in excellent order. Some think its style is out of harmony but it reminds me of many similar ones in the *skjærgård* of islands which stretches for hundreds of miles along the Norwegian coast that I look on it with pleasure.

Rex Herdman in his memoirs describes 'a perfect island for hide and seek. The grazing was prized as richer grass than sandy Rutland.'

The Herdmans sold it, in 1935, to a Dublin barrister. Their faithful boatman and caretaker Broom and his wife had retired and coming and going was more difficult. Then it passed to a pair of English ladies, Doctor Mayo and Dentist Sharp, who came there in June and September for many years.

They launched their boat on a certain day and there was no shortage of helpers as generous refreshments were on tap – and again for the hauling up. The sight of those two amiable ladies at ease in deck chairs on the wooden veranda is such an abiding memory that I feel sure their spirits haunt the island still.

Beside the house now is a seawater swimming pool usable at low water when the sands are dry. Beyond it are rocky hillocks with hidden precipices and sudden hollows – hard going for the walker but ideal shelter for nurturing trees and shrubs. These have been generously planted and will soon,

one hopes, add an arboretum to an archipelago which has hardly more than scarce stunted bushes elsewhere.

Inishcoo

You can walk across to this sister island of Edernish at low water. The sandy sound is narrow and now little used but, before the days of engines, boats found it a handy short cut at high water to avoid the strong tides in the main channel. 'Coo is shaped like a lozenge, a half chewed one. The name means Isle of Greyhounds – perhaps it is where the great O'Donnell, Lords of the Isles, kennelled them and also five-foot high Irish wolfhounds.

The handsome wall, which zigzags across the island near its southern end, may have been built, on the foundation of an older one, to protect islanders or stock from houndish rapacity.

The surface of 'Coo, like the shoreline, is knobbly with bits of rock, small marshes and a lovely lake, as Ros has depicted. It is grand for a bathe or a bath and is shared via a congested bridge with Eighter.

The heyday of Inishcoo, like Rutland, lay in the late 18th and early 19th Centuries when the herring were running up the sound bent on suicide like lemming. But it also had a more recent period of activity after 1890 when 100 ton schooners were being built in the cove facing the channel. Sails were sewn and roped for them and nets knitted in an adjoining loft. A Congested Herring and Mackerel Curing Station in 1891 was opened and big catches landed. By this time steam trawlers were joining in and the hoots of their sirens and whistles as they demanded space alongside added to the din.

Picture pyramids of new barrels waiting to be filled beside rows of full and branded ones ready to be winched into the yawning holds of steamers bound for God knows where. Spare a dash of pity too for local boats arriving, under sail, late in the day finding the bidding over because barrels or the salt had run out and having to dump their catch into the sea.

Coo House, conspicuous today by its handsome appearance and wedge-shaped gable, looks over the narrow sound towards Edernish. For many years it was the Coastguard Officer's residence. In the 1950s several brothers, nicknamed the Kitties after their mother, lived there. Captain Dominic O'Donnell, who commanded Irish ships during the war and sometimes joined British convoys for security, usually wore a peaked pilot cap. It was rumoured that his local knowledge had saved coastal convoys by taking them close inshore where U boats couldn't follow.

Frank, whose house we saw on Eighter, would often be there of an evening. 'Charlie Mary Kitty' combined the offices of Harbour Pilot and lobster fisherman. Both occupations require a detailed knowledge of underwater rocks and he was most helpful at the time we were gathering information for the first yacht guide to the west coast. His

Inishcoo

lean weather-beaten face and stiff jaw under a worn cloth cap became pleasantly familiar.

Charlie often broke into a smile to relate a good story in the midst of explaining various approaches to the land.

One was of a County Antrim drifter skipper who, like others from Rutland, went to church on Aranmore. The sermon was about faith and how St Paul had saved the Cyprus ship from foundering. 'The shipmen cast four anchors over the stern and wished for the dawn.' It was too much for the captain. Thumping his stick on the floor he loudly declared. "Dom bod seamanship. They should' a put them over the boo."

My favourite was of Teague O'Boyle, a local pilot who rose to command his own coaster. Leaving Dublin with the hold full of beer and whiskey the crew became weather-bound at Skerries. This is the port where they ate Saint Patrick's goat and have never been allowed to forget about it. So inhabitants retaliate with liquid hospitality. Teague's crew felt they had to respond and decided to broach the cargo.
"The whole of Skerries was then drunk for three weeks".
The storyteller paused in envy of that glorious interlude.
"Now in them days hanging was the penalty for broaching cargo, so Teague had to lose the ship to save his neck. He picked a rock out there in the sound that no one else knew about. With the drink still on him, he had to tack three times to find it. But down she went!"

Another, undoubtedly true, was of a blanket he'd hung out to dry on the island.

It wasn't there when he returned and islanders, poachers and passing fishermen were questioned in turn, to no avail. But when his cow calved a fortnight later the blanket was inside neatly folded. She swallowed it to keep the calf warm!

Edward McCarron, the lightkeeper, tells us in his memoirs of the shebeen on Rutland in 1880. The lady who ran it was often in trouble with the Coastguards from 'Coo, whereas the shebeen on Aran was not bothered because the police stationed on the island got their drink there at prices lower than in the Pub.

8. Inishfree, Illancrone and Roaninish

Inishfree

Inishfree Upper is a pancake about three quarters of a mile in diameter and rising no more than 60 feet. Its name, one of the commonest among Irish and Scottish islands, means Heather Isle but its centre, as Ros depicts, is so covered in rocks – round, knobbly, split, sloping or smooth – as to leave little room for ling. Seaweed grows long and thick on the tide line.

So Inishfree has been described as rich in kelp, short on grazing. Goemoniers, as they call seaweed croppers in Brittany, could settle there and make a rich living. At the south end, on patches of white sand, curious blackened tree stumps survive. Their bare roots spread out ten feet or more like the legs of spiders. High tides covering them with salt and reefs that shelter them from big breakers may have led to the extraordinary survival of what appear to have been giant cedars.

When June and I first visited in 1958, Patrick Duffy greeted us at the door of his two storey house. Over a cup of tea he told us he was 72 and had never been off the island "except to the Port, and once to Cork."

The community then stood at 50 but the problem was retaining a school when there were only five children. They tried having the teacher on the mainland and boating the children half a mile south to Crohy but "it didn't work right."

"There was fair grazing on the island this year but we put cattle which needed fattening up on to Inishallya." That is 'Inishal' on the chart, adjoining at low water.

Patsy, his tall handsome son, came in with his Belfast-born bride Margaret. They showed us a ten pound lobster he'd just caught. It must gave been twenty years old and tough eating, but would fetch a good price ashore. Tales followed about ring netting for herring. Coming in after dark, by the tortuous channel north of the island, he had a code of torch signals to let Margaret know if he had a catch to unload at the factory at the Port or was coming to the island pier.

"You can get a doctor over from Burtonport in 20 minutes and Father Mulloy, although he's 85, would be here as quick but they can't get to the outer isles and that's what's drives old people to come to live on the mainland."

tle religion but favoured drumming and semi-nude dancing. They grew a few vegetables but didn't seem too keen on 'Good Life' husbandry finding the State un-employment allowance adequate. The native islanders were tolerant but recalled that the hippies failed to pull their weight in looking after roads, paths and all-important drains. After 19 years of it, as all grew older, island pleasures waned and they just moved away.

In 2002 Liam Miller, skipper of the beautiful wooden cutter *Manutara*, took us to Inishfree in his sixteen foot tender, steering expertly through reefs off the pier. Forty years on there was no fishing and the cattle were mainland owned. Good news was of mains electricity and water being piped across and more people moving in. Best of all was a warm welcome from Margaret Duffy – just as if we'd never been away! She was sitting on the lawn where she'd left one area of grass uncut to encourage wild flowers like king cups and hawksbit.

Her cottage was full of her daughter Maraid's paintings and a seaweed montage of great originality. Preparations were being made for an island Art Festival a few weeks ahead. Listening to these plans and wishing I had time to join in, there arose a feeling that Inishfree has found an important artistic niche among the islands of the 21st Century.

Preserved tree stumps on beach on Inishfree

Seeing us off at the pier he described the ten-foot dinghy we'd arrived in as 'comical'. That must have been how it looked, with two tall people and an outboard weighing it down until the gunwhale was only inches above the water. Best of all was his parting remark, "This is the best island I've ever heard of to live on."

It might also be said to have the best literary account of any. The novel *Islanders* by Paedar O'Donnell, the Inishfree schoolmaster, brilliantly evokes the joys and sorrows of earlier days. Special for me is the account, based on fact, of the perilous voyage by the hero Charlie Dougan in a winter gale. After three failed efforts by the strongest on the island to launch wooden boats, he got his paddling currach lifted onto the back of a receding wave and fought through rows of breakers. Then it was a race downwind to get the doctor for a woman in labour.

Not long after our visit a group of hippies took over five houses. A woman was their chief. Her followers showed lit-

Illancrone

This is a bouldery reef just six hundred yards long and fifteen feet high. It occupies a key position at the south entrance to Aranmore roadstead, a mile east of Inishfree. The light at the extreme south end of the outlying reefs is a welcome sight on dark nights to returning fishing boats.

In Scotland they define an island as being big enough to hold one family, or feed a sheep. By this standard Crone rates as a mere rock. But it is a marginal case.

On this salubrious spot are the vestiges of three stone huts, now used to store kelp. For us Crone merits inclusion as a Hermitage used by St. Crona Beg (Wee Crona). She came in summer only, for waves would regularly sweep all over it in winter.

Picture Crona as 5th Century Mother Teresa, a peripatetic preacher who had her own church on the Termon peninsula a mile east of Illancrone. Her name is revered locally on Cruit Island; but also far afield in Mayo at Killalla and many other places.

On silken silent summer mornings Crona would have rowed her tiny currach out here and prayed until she reached a tranquil state of mind.

Roaninish

'Seal Island' as the name means, or Roanish as it is colloquially called, lies about four miles west-nor-west of Inniskeel. I've never heard of anybody living on it, but fishermen in the old days must have often camped there when tending long lines and pots. It is covered in short grass and is almost flat.

We landed on it in 1959, curious to examine a wreck. This was the *Greenhaven*, a steel coaster which must have had the luckiest crew ever. She had discharged a cargo of 'bagstuff' fertiliser at Killalla and was returning north with no cargo, 'light' as sailors say, and that was her salvation. The engine packed up and she drifted helpless before a westerly gale. At dawn on the height of a big spring tide a giant wave threw her on her side onto a flat outer reef . As the waters fell, the crew, bruised but otherwise unharmed, were able to step onto the rocks dry shod . She lay there still like a toy boat with little sign of damage. If my crew were hoping for loot they were disappointed. Everything to the last safety pin had been removed. Months later I was coyly offered the skipper's sextant for a fiver!

Inishkeel

One August Saturday evening *Wild Goose* lay tugging at her anchor chain in the horseshoe cove known as Church Bay at the east end of Inishkeel. No more than half a mile long and sixty feet high, it lies just north of the pleasant holiday resort of Portnoo. The intriguing scents of the island came across on a puff of wind – the milky smell of cows, turf smoke from a fisherman's fire, crushed crab from a pile of nets, a whiff of sweetness from Ladies Bedstraw.

After stowing the sails, June and I rowed ashore to explore. A full moon rose at dusk and *Wild Goose* appeared as a black silhouette against a silver sea, her harmonic lines matching the curve of the beach.

> *'A ship, an isle, a sickle moon, with few*
> *but with how splendid stars'*

To our right the low walls of St. Mary's and St. Conall's churches and some high tombstones threw long moon shadows over grass the colour of pewter. A sense of tranquillity enfolded the scene. The only place that has affected me to the same extent is Iona.

In the morning we rowed across to Portnoo and climbed the steep path up to the church. The Bishop of Derry and Raphoe started his sermon by saying how lucky most of the congregation were, like himself, to be on holiday in Portnoo. He then spoke of the many saintly connections of the area.

During the service the wind had been gusting up and now made the window rattle. I'm always uneasy when *Wild Goose* is out of sight in a blow and began to wonder if she was dragging her anchor. The Bishop warmed to his theme and looking over his right shoulder mentioned the yacht – an unusual sight in those days. He could see her from the height of the pulpit. It took some restraint not to put my hand up and say, "Please, My Lord, is she still in the bay where we left her?" But I held my peace and, when we emerged into the sunlight, all was well. The tide was falling and in another hour we could have walked across to the green oval isle spread below us like a water lily.

This islet became, in the 6th Century A.D., the most important religious centre in all Donegal. The physical evidence lies in the ruins we had glimpsed the previous night and in many unique carved slabs lying around them.

The origins of St. Conall are obscure, and myths are many, but it is clear that he earned widespread veneration and affection in his own lifetime. A simplistic view is that the importance of Inishkeel began after Conall, born c. 500 A.D., killed his father in a fit of temper. Seven years of self-imposed penance followed, sleeping on a stone bed and eating limpets on deserted Inishkeel. Feeling the need of company Conall then gathered together some monkish friends. Their association led to the founding of a monastic community of wattle huts where others could come for spiritual comfort. Conall is usually given the soubriquet *Caol.* This might come from the Gaelic *keel,* meaning a strait and referring to the narrows which divide island and mainland. His name is, I believe, borne by Donegal's most dangerous rocks, the Ballyconnel Blowers a mile outside Gola. *Bally* appears to be a chart maker's distortion of *bullig,* which usually means a belly or reef. The restless swell breaks forever on those rocks so the nomenclature is appropriate to Conall's fiery nature.

Conall or Connel grew in importance to become second only to his contemporary and cousin St. Columba. Blood was spilt in 590 when St. Dallan, a close friend of Conall's, arrived to interpret manuscripts. Although blind, Dallan was famed as the leading literary man of his day - no mean title at a time when Irish monasteries were respected far afield as the sole repositories of learning in a Europe mired in the Dark Ages. When pirates came ashore Dallan may have upset them by mouthing the wrong sort of verse

because they chopped off his head and threw it into the sea. A prayer from Connel brought it back to the surface. The two are said to be buried in the same grave on Inishkeel. Perhaps some day the two skeletons will be discovered.

There was a right royal row on the island in A.D. 619, recorded much later in the *Annals of the Four Masters of* Donegal town. In 619 Doir, son of the High King of Ireland, was slain on Inishkeel by Failbhe Flann, King of Munster. The cause has been forgotten but the presence of kings and princes indicates the importance of the island.

On one such warlike occasion the original monastic buildings must have been destroyed. Those we see today are mediaeval but the inscribed stones are earlier. Most striking is a Maltese cross with below it two figures in a chariot, perhaps a link with sun worship. The first Irish Christians made accommodation with earlier beliefs and as a result Ireland was converted without a martyr. It is curious that, in contrast to Scottish carvings, none on Inishkeel depicts a boat or galley.

In mediaeval days, members of the ruling Donegal families Gallagher, O'Neill, Doherty, O' Boyle and McSweeny would have come regularly here to do penance and pray for victory in their perpetual wars. Red Hugh O'Donnell must have been here walking the ling like a buck in spring, accompanied by his scheming mother Ineenduv, to give thanks for his escape from Dublin Castle. She had, by

Inishkeel from Portnoo

means of an accomplice, smuggled in a rope on which he slid down the walls.

In the 18th Century Inishkeel became a centre of walks known as Turas in which pilgrims walked from one station to another saying prayers at each on the island and those on the adjoining mainland. In 1835 these became occasions of amusement and drinking so were suppressed by the clergy.

The Barretts, the last family to live on the island came ashore in 1904. The remains of their dwelling house can be seen and they still graze the land. Sand levels in the sound vary but in 2002 it is accessible on foot around each low water.

Formal worship is now intermittent but the spiritual strength will remain forever,

As o'er each continent and island
The dawn leads on another day
The voice of prayer is never silent
Nor dies the strain of praise away

(Hymn)

Rathlin O'Birne

Beyond the long arm of the law
Close to a shipping road
Pirates in their pirate lairs
Observe their pirate code.

Auden

O'Birne is about three-quarters of a mile long and 100 feet high. Lying a mile off the most westerly point of Donegal, it is far enough out to make the voyage in an open boat exciting. There are jagged reefs at either end and, the day we went, fog was sliding down the 2000 foot slopes of Slieve League astern, threatening to hide the island. Having failed to get south in *Agivey* with sea conditions right for landing we got a lift out with a friendly boatman from Malinbeg.

In the morning light Rathlin O'Birne looked like an old starving lion lying flat on its tummy, showing bones through its threadbare skin. In a dry summer, when the grass withers, the lion's back is tawny; in a wet one it is green like the cloak of Judah. The approach to the island is through the lion's jaws at the southern end. There gapes a U-shaped cove with eighty-foot cliffs on either hand, a landing place as dramatic as Malinbeg. The cliffs vary in

colour like a lion's mane — patches with the rusty glow of corrugated iron, others camel, dun and silver. Lower down they are black with the patchy lichen, which loves to grow on sheltered shorelines in an even band just above high water. Here the line is blurry and spatter-dashed because of the habitual roughness of the Atlantic swell. At the inner end of the cove where the cliffs narrow to sixty feet apart you find a concrete pier and a series of slippery steps. When raiding parties arrived to raid cattle from the 'Northmen' of Donegal mainland, it was here they hid their galleys.

If you don't fancy the steps there is a vertical steel ladder set tight to the cliff face. The Dublin Ballast Board built these and the pier when the lighthouse was first opened in 1865. If you find yourself short of breath climbing up, just think of the labour involved in humping up bags of potatoes and oil drums to supply the light keepers and their families. To make this work less arduous a wire rope used to be stretched taut across the top of the gut with a slider on it known as a Flying Fox. When the sea was too rough for a step's landing, men and materials were hauled out of a boat in the middle of the gut, then slid across to a concrete landing pad.

At the wall's end is a different hazard for walkers – a storm beach of rounded boulders bigger than footballs over which a way must be carefully picked. This moraine, created by seas breaking clean across, extends in a graduation of smaller stones, pebbles and shingle down to the eastern shoreline. Just beyond are signs of lazy beds on a south-facing slope and what looked like the gables of a house.

To our right, from here, there is a small stone pier, encumbered with rocks at low water, for landings when the south cove is inaccessible. Inland of this, extended arcs and semi-circles of tumbled stones show, probably marking the boundary of a 6th Century monastic clachan. Near the shore are a roofed-in Holy Well, an open-air altar and a couple of beehive huts. The fact that all is so overgrown adds a degree of mysticism.

There are very strong saintly connections. St. Assicus or Tassagh, a coppersmith by trade, spent seven years here in self-imposed hermitage. He later went to care for St. Patrick on his deathbed. The name O'Birne is said to come from his contemporary, who frequented these parts – Hugh McBric. A useful man to have around. He was so good at curing headaches that I wonder why the aspirin boys don't use him as a Patron. But he affected some cures by transferring the pain to himself, which might not suit their advertising patter.

Rathlin O'Birne Light

I arrived that way on my first visit and the keepers seemed to be more concerned to give an easy landing to their foodstuffs than a mere visitor like me. Steadying up I soon found that the chances of a tumble didn't end. Little Johnny Head-in-Air wouldn't keep his feet for long on this island as the surface is pitted with hidden holes made by rabbits and nesting birds. The safest way to the eastern shore is along the path between the massive twin walls of granite, which lead north from the lighthouse buildings. These, in days before electronic aids to navigation, were kept whitewashed as a day mark for passing ships. Now they have a luxuriant coat of lichen, encouraged by the least polluted air in Europe.

Rathlin O'Birne Landing

There are two other Irish islands called Rathlin. The one off Ballycastle, County Antrim, and Lambay anciently called *Reachra*, off Malahide. An expert whom I consulted in 1980 concluded that Rathlin meant a 'saw-edge', hence a rough-shored island, which would suit all three. He hazarded a guess that the 'birne' could come from the red granite. Some of O'Birne's rocks, we saw, are as red as a boiled lobster.

There could be another link. Rathlin, County Antrim, had a resident giant called Finn McCool who was handy with a hammer. If you walk up to the west side of O'Birne you'll see dozens of red rocks split as if with a two hundred pounder, quite unlike the rounded ones of the storm beach. Who but a giant did it?

Other saints like Brendan, Columcille or Cormac the Navigator must have called here on their frequent coasting voyages. It is such an obvious staging point on which to fill up water skins or stretch cramped legs after the 40 mile crossing of Donegal Bay.

Listen in the island's delightful silence for the ring of Assicus' hammer as he produced copper monastic bells, the scratch of Columcille's pen illuminating a manuscript while awaiting a fair wind, or Brendan's scalpel as he carved a sun compass for the next ocean voyage.

Raids occurred. In 1542 an O'Flaherty longship from Clare Island arrived, bent on plunder. An instant attack by

Turlough McSweeny surprised and slew all the crew except for the leader. He, son of The O'Flaherty, was returned home unhurt. Such were the conventions of the time.

Later the O'Birnes left their spoils of war guarded only by an 80 and a 16 year old. MacSweenys from Aranmore learned of this and made a dawn approach. Luckily, the lad spotted them and set sail for help. The McFaddens of Doran were glad to oblige and at dawn next day made an unseen approach out of the rising sun.

The MacSweenys, after an enjoyable 24 hours torturing the old O'Birne to persuade him to reveal the treasure, were taken by surprise and killed except, again, for the leader who was set at liberty. All right for some!

At the north end Ros spotted some unusual limpet shells beside a rock, which served as a lookout for a lordly Black Back Gull. Their surfaces were encrusted to an unusual extent with tiny mussel shells and barnacles in a lively pattern. She later framed a montage of several of exceptional beauty to hang in her studio. Ros also found beauty in a hawk's cast. It consisted of a spillikin of tiny bones and fur, bleached and welded together by sun and wind. So she framed that too. You can see it in her studio!

Our walk concluded with a visit to the highest point of the island. From here a lookout for passing ships would have been maintained. There are traces of the defensive wall and ditch of a cashel. The port, seen from above, looked like the crater of a volcano with one side knocked out.

When we visited, maintenance men were at work on the solar panels that now provide power for the Light. Only an occasional boost is needed from a diesel generator. The fitters were convinced that the tower contains a ghost who will call out your name if you are up top alone, maybe the spirit of a drowned sailor. It wouldn't surprise me — there have been many shipwrecks and ten men have died in collision with the island's rocks in the last thirty years.

The fitters showed us the massive stand where a nuclear power pack once stood with a half-life of twenty years. It proved uneconomic and was removed at half time. Removed too, after 1912, were the lightkeeper's families who had lived here with their men folk from around 1875 until 1912. After that the men got a good deal with four weeks on the island and four weeks on leave ashore in each two-month period. That lasted for some eighty years. Now sadly, Rathlin O'Birne like all other Irish Lights is unmanned and automatic. The fitters were going home by helicopter at 5pm, having put in a 35 hour week like city men.

O'Birne is not as far from the mainland as Inishtrahull but is, perhaps, more isolated because it lacks the Hull's superb natural harbour. There is no record of a fishing and farming community as existed on the Hull up until 1927. The most numerous visitors today are barnacle geese — beautiful but

greedy feeders. They alight by the thousand in winter to the dismay of sheep owners.

Rathlin O'Birne has its own distinctive atmosphere which it would take more than one visit to absorb.

Innishmurray

Old saints on millstones float with cats
To islands out at sea
Whereon no female pelvis can
Threaten their agapee.

W.H. Auden

This important isle lies just south of the inter county border so is in fact part of Sligo, but it seems to group better with the Donegal islands as there is not another habitable one for 50 miles west. Low-lying, a mile long by half that in width it is like a mini edition of Tory.

After a couple of unsuccessful tries to get to it by yacht in the stormy summer of 2002 we were taken out for a most reasonable fee by a Mullaghmore boatman in the stout cruiser boat he built with his own hands. The voyage out past Classiebawn Castle where Lord Mountbatten used to summer, took a bit over an hour. We got a good view of the curious apron of flat rock which runs most of the way round the shoreline, a hunting ground for kelp and winkles. The landing place at Clashymore is a rockbound gut facing southwest into the prevailing wind. June and I discovered this when anchored there on what appeared a settled evening in 1965. Waves hissing alongside and the breeze blowing straight onto the rocks woke us at midnight. After some anxious moments of checking bearings and cables, the holding proved good and we postponed departure until dawn.

One is surprised not by the fact that this inish is now uninhabited but that it supported a population of fifty or more for so many centuries. Bronze Age people came here for the fishing. They, or their successors, built a strong stone cashel which sticks up in the middle like a conning tower. Well, sort of like a conning tower. Perhaps it was this that decided a destroyer captain in 1916 to torpedo the island, thinking it was a U-boat! 'A very natural mistake.' one might say but, calculating the price of torpedoes, his Admiral was unsympathetic.

In the 6th Century A.D. monks led by St. Columba himself took over, perhaps from Druids, and augmented the cashel. 'Murray has seen raids by Vikings and Normans and watched Armada galleons seek shelter in her lee, until cables broke and hulls were shattered on Streedagh strand.

In 1779 there were only five families; according to a contemporary fishery report they lived by selling their catch on the mainland. They inter-married and claimed to have been in possession for 700 years.

Despite its small size and isolation, in common with all the Donegal islands, Inishmurray should not be considered cut off from the outside world. Between the World Wars Michael Waters, the King, put two sons through Trinity

Donegal Bay on the way to Innishmurray

College, Dublin. One son, John, served as a captain in the British army in World War II and later practised as an accountant from the family house, Mount Temple in Grange. John was tragically drowned while bathing from the beach behind the house in 1967. His brother, Michael, became a noted lobster exporter.

The island was evacuated in 1947 but as in most cases there was much to and fro movement thereafter. Janette Eccles, who lived near Milk Harbour, used to supply some comforts to island people in a cave they kept furnished at Streedagh. This was for use when held up by weather on their way to the island. They came and went mostly from the open beach. Only consummate sailors could do that with safety.

Jan, a fearless sailor herself who crewed often with me, upset the island once by approaching the harbour north about. She arrived to find a flurry of activity as stills were being hidden and kegs stowed away. The use of this route was a signal that a gauger was on board!

The long history of poteen manufacture and its place as a mainstay of Inishmurray's economy is evidenced in the Memoirs of Sam Waters, a Royal Irish Constabulary Officer. He describes how he thought that a spell of still frosty weather just before Christmas 1866 would be a good time to make a raid. Five coast guards and four police-men landed at dawn and had a successful search. But

Natural harbours at Innishmurray

The Cashel on Innishmurray

that evening the weather broke and they had to stay on. Camping in the schoolhouse they purchased turf and made do with hens, ducks and potatoes but had to sleep on the floor and not one had a change of clothing. The Queen was so kind to them that before leaving ten days later they returned most of the worms and wash they had seized. Her Majesty then presented Sam with some vintage stuff she kept for the family. This was sampled using eggshells for glasses. She apologised saying that at a recent dance a fight had broken out and every item of glass and crockery in her house been smashed! Next time we are short of glasses for a party at home I must remember that excuse.

In 2002 we walked to the cashel along a narrow footpath with benny weed so high and thick that our white pants were coloured bright yellow from the flowers. The soil must be rich to grow it that tall but no animals were grazing the island. They say adequate shepherding is impossible and the growing of crops must always have been difficult with no hill to protect from gales. They had to tether the cabbages!

The thick walls of the cashel are impressive but it would have taken forty men at least to hold the perimeter against a raiding galley crew. If it was defence the builders wanted why did they not build, like Tory, a round tower? That properly provisioned could have held out forever. Perhaps the walls were to keep mischievous monks in, not Vikings out.

The collection of carvings and buildings in the cashel is unique and well catalogued elsewhere. As a passing visitor I find it better not to get involved in admiring the detail. By doing so one risks losing the sense of wonder at the fervour of worship that filled this place for many lifetimes. Better to let imagination recreate the busy life of a monastic day – livestock to be cared for, fish to be salted, ink and medicines to be manufactured, manuscripts copied and illuminated, prayers to be said beside the outdoor altars, a lookout day and night kept for approaching ships – all this as well as periods of meditation in the dark cells.

My recollections of our visit are twofold: a feeling of time warp from sitting on the stone bench built into the structure of the beehive known as the schoolhouse and the yawning mouths of baby swallows in a niche in the roof rocks of another dark beehive.

The latter day schoolhouse at the east end of the row of houses has been taken over for the display of selected stones and carvings. A well-informed lecturer was inside telling adult students about the island's history.

Going back towards the port we passed three Board of Works men replacing soil disturbed by archaeologists in a small graveyard by a Station of the Cross on the south shore. They told us how yesterday in warm rain they'd been eaten by midges. Today with a breeze there was no problem.

Theirs were the only signs of active archaeology we'd seen in a summer of island visiting.

As we bathed in the natural seawater pool left by the tide near the harbour and ate our picnic lunch in sunshine, we'd had a most satisfying and enjoyable day.

Innishmurray appears from one viewpoint untidy and neglected, from another an unrivalled site in which to bring alive for students the old Celtic Church at one of the most beautiful periods in Christian history. Welsh islands like Skokholm and Ramsay have partially solved the problem of caretaking by having bird watchers and wardens as summer residents. Their islands are close to the coast, which makes it easier, but in the medium term some such arrangement would be of enormous benefit to Innishmurray.

Epilogue

'Great days in the distance enchanted
Days of fresh air in the rain and the sun'

We are all creatures of the open air – our ancestors were content to rove forests and mountains. The smarter ones moved to islands as providing bigger and better caves to live in, fish as food and the natural boundaries which were doubly valuable before the days of barbed wire for fencing.

This is the oldest reason for the attraction of islands. Those so attracted became sailors and so attracted more. Walter de la Mare noted,

'Every seaman, every wanderer on the deep, has hearkened
to the decoy of that ideal island… and where is the lands-
man with soul so dead that has never caught its enchanting
echo?'

I agree, not as an island dweller but an island rover. Since my good father first carried me, aged five, over the bow of a fishing boat onto a rocky skerry, I have never been able to resist an island on the horizon. This has lead to a lot of fun, visiting more than two hundred European isles in fifty years of sailing *Wild Goose* and her consorts.

But no time is like the first time and I still love Donegal islands best. What is special about them? They contain no fortification built later than about 600 A.D. Compare that with Mediterranean or Brittany coasts which were raided so often that villages had to move ten miles inland and every headland and coastal hill bears a fort. The Vikings came to Donegal – and went – without much trace. Sheephaven is counted as the only Viking sea name.

Others raided too. About 1800 a boat's crew from Ness in Lewis went missing and were assumed to have been drowned. Years later survivors were found enslaved in Africa. The same Barbary pirates would have been delighted, en passant, to pick up a Tory crew but Donegal was relatively untroubled by sea-borne raids. Sea and wind were enemies enough.

Another was the County Council, often with conniv-ance of the Church and anxious to save money on services, subsidies and unemployment allowances. Their efforts, with specious offers of property on the mainland, closed down several communities. Now the Council are big friends, pip-ing electricity and water out to help meet the ever increasing demand for holiday homes.

Donegal isles have more than their share of Christian faith. Eight of those we visited have active churches, early church ruins, complete church clachans, holy wells or penitential stations. Donegal monks lived in charity with their island neighbours, not isolated on barely accessible rock like brothers further south on The Skelligs or High Island. All face rough seas, all remain unspoilt, all like being visited.

That's enough of analysis - islands are like pretty girls: to be admired, loved, enjoyed but never really understood. As W. S. Bristowe remarked in his splendid *Book of Islands* (G. Bell and Sons 1969),

'Leave taking will incite a thirst for another island where hidden treasures or fresh ways of life may be found.'

Even should my life yield no more I am content — the past has given enough.

Cottage

Publications

Cottage Publications
is an imprint of
Laurel Cottage Ltd
15 Ballyhay Road
Donaghadee, Co. Down
N. Ireland, BT21 0NG

Dear Reader

This book is from our much complimented illustrated book series which includes:-

Belfast
By the Lough's North Shore
East Belfast
South Belfast
Antrim, Town & Country
Inishowen
Donegal Highlands
Donegal, South of the Gap
Donegal Islands
Fermanagh
Omagh
Cookstown
Dundalk & North Louth

Drogheda & the Boyne Valley
Blanchardstown, Castleknock and the Park
Dundrum, Stillorgan & Rathfarnham
Blackrock, Dún Laoghaire, Dalkey
Limerick's Glory
Galway on the Bay
The Book of Clare
Armagh
Ring of Gullion
The Mournes
Heart of Down
Strangford Shores

For the more athletically minded our illustrated walking book series includes:-

Bernard Davey's Mourne
Bernard Davey's Mourne Part 2

Tony McAuley's Glens

Also available in our 'Illustrated History & Companion' Range are:-

City of Derry
Lisburn

Holywood
Banbridge

Ballymoney

And from our Music series:-

Colum Sands, Between the Earth and the Sky

We can also supply prints, individually signed by the artist, of the paintings featured in the above titles as well as many other areas of Ireland.

For details on these superb publications and to view samples of the paintings they contain, you can visit our web site at **www.cottage-publications.com** or alternatively you can contact us as follows:-

Telephone: +44 (028) 9188 8033

Fax: +44 (028) 9188 8063